GCSE RELIGIOUS STUDIES
A STUDY OF THE GOSPEL OF MARK

Colourpoint
Educational

Rewarding Learning

Juliana Gilbride

ISBN: 978 1 906578 35 0

First Edition
Third Impression, 2014

Layout and design: April Sky Design
Printed by: GPS Colour Graphics Ltd, Belfast

The Author

Juliana Gilbride, B.Ed
(Hons), M.Ed, was part of
a team of teachers who
revised the Religious
Studies GCSE Specification
for CCEA (for first teaching
in 2009). She is a Revisor
for GCSE Religious Studies
for CCEA, and has fifteen
years experience of
teaching Religious Studies
in Northern Ireland.

COLOURPOINT
EDUCATIONAL

Colourpoint Educational
An imprint of Colourpoint Creative Ltd
Colourpoint House
Jubilee Business Park
21 Jubilee Road
Newtownards
County Down
Northern Ireland
BT23 4YH

Tel: 028 9182 6339
Fax: 028 9182 1900
E-mail: info@colourpoint.co.uk
Web site: www.colourpoint.co.uk

Acknowledgements

The acknowledgements on page 70 constitute an
extension of this copyright page.

CONTENTS

CHAPTER 5 THE DEATH AND RESURRECTION OF JESUS 45

CHAPTER 6 THE ROLE AND NATURE OF CHRISTIAN DISCIPLESHIP 57

For your folder   In a Group   Further Thinking

Chapter 1

BACKGROUND TO MARK'S GOSPEL

The word 'Gospel' means 'good news'. It is comes from the Anglo-Saxon *god spel*, which can mean 'spell it out', 'speak out' or 'proclaim'. In the Bible the Gospels proclaim the good news about Jesus. There are four Gospels with four different writers: Matthew, Mark, Luke and John.

Each records the events of Jesus' life, death and Resurrection. Three of the Gospels – Matthew, Mark and Luke – are very similar in content and structure. These are called the 'Synoptic Gospels'. The word *synoptic* means 'shared view'. Many passages from these three Gospels can be placed side by side to show how similar they are. For example, the story of Jesus' baptism and temptations (Matthew 3:13–4:11, Mark 1:9-13, Luke 3:19-4:19). The fourth account of Jesus' life, John's Gospel, is very different in style and content to the other three.

After Jesus' death, Resurrection and Ascension, many stories circulated about him. His disciples and close friends would have recalled incidents that other people would know nothing of. Each group of people would probably have remembered different events. At first these stories about Jesus were passed around by word of mouth. This is known as the '**Christian Oral Tradition**'.

Many of the early Christians believed that Jesus would return during their lifetime (the idea that Jesus will return is called the 'second coming' or *parousia*.) However, as time passed, those first Christians who had met Jesus began to die out. It was important that the stories about Jesus were preserved, so they were written down.

Besides the four Gospels included in the New Testament, there are a number of other documents that claim to give written accounts of Jesus' life. These other accounts have not been accepted by the Church and are considered unreliable. Often they are written far too long after the event to be trusted.

The Gospel writers are called 'evangelists', that is, those who spread the good news about Jesus. Each writer tells the story of Jesus' life and death in their own unique way.

It would be too simple to describe the Gospels as 'biographies' of Jesus. You won't find many details on what Jesus looked like or what he did when he was growing up. Instead, the Gospel writers focused on the things that were important to them.

FACTS ABOUT THE GOSPELS

No one is certain when the Gospels first emerged. You might assume that Matthew's Gospel is the earliest book in the New Testament, because it comes first. However, if you look at the **timeline** you will realise that Paul's letters, such as Romans and Corinthians, seem to be the earliest books. Most scholars argue that Mark's Gospel, the shortest one, was the first to appear (around AD64–65).

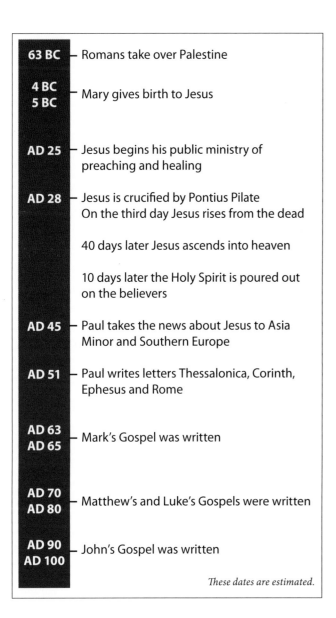

63 BC	Romans take over Palestine
4 BC **5 BC**	Mary gives birth to Jesus
AD 25	Jesus begins his public ministry of preaching and healing
AD 28	Jesus is crucified by Pontius Pilate On the third day Jesus rises from the dead
	40 days later Jesus ascends into heaven
	10 days later the Holy Spirit is poured out on the believers
AD 45	Paul takes the news about Jesus to Asia Minor and Southern Europe
AD 51	Paul writes letters Thessalonica, Corinth, Ephesus and Rome
AD 63 **AD 65**	Mark's Gospel was written
AD 70 **AD 80**	Matthew's and Luke's Gospels were written
AD 90 **AD 100**	John's Gospel was written

These dates are estimated.

Who was Mark?

Mark, sometimes called 'John Mark' is mentioned a lot in the New Testament. Most scholars believe that he is the author of Mark's Gospel. We know that he lived in Jerusalem (Acts 12:12) and that he was probably a Greek-speaking Jew (a Hellenist). Mark was not one of the twelve apostles, although he seems to have been a good friend of the apostle Peter. Many scholars believe that Peter's preaching provided Mark with much of his material. Mark also set out with Paul on his First Missionary Journey (Acts 12:25).

THE PURPOSE OF MARK'S GOSPEL

The four Gospels, Matthew, Mark, Luke and John, tell us about the life of Jesus. Each has a different emphasis which shows us what was important to the author and his readers. Each Gospel writer or evangelist had a 'target audience' in mind when writing his Gospel.

Some people believe that Mark was written at the time when Christians were suffering persecution under the reign of the Roman Emperor Nero, and that he was writing for the persecuted Christians. A third of the Gospel focuses on Jesus' suffering and death. Readers of the Gospel are advised to *"take up your cross and follow me" (Mark 8:34-35)*, which suggests that they may have been under the threat of persecution.

CHARACTERISTICS OF MARK'S GOSPEL

• **Style**

The style of Mark's Gospel is simple, brief and blunt. Mark does not waste words but gets straight to the point. It is the shortest of the four Gospels.

There are very few references made to the Jewish scriptures and Jewish customs are explained, which suggests that Mark was writing for a Gentile (non-Jewish) audience. Mark also explains the meaning of any words that he quotes in Aramaic, the language used in Palestine at the time.

FOR YOUR FOLDER

Look up the following verses and pick out the Aramaic word used by Mark along with the English translation:

Reference	Aramaic word/phrase	Translation
3:17		
5:41		
7:34		
15:22		
15:34		

• An eye-witness account

Another characteristic of Mark's Gospel is that on a number of occasions it seems that an eye-witness must have been present at events. For example, there may be a particular emphasis on an exact detail. Many scholars believe that the eye-witness was the apostle Peter who was a close friend of Mark's.

FOR YOUR FOLDER

Look up the following verses and note the detail that Mark gives which suggests he is describing an eye-witness account:

Reference	Detail
4:35 - 38	
6:39	
10:32	
10:50	

• Failure

Jesus' disciples left everything to follow him. However, throughout Mark's Gospel we are reminded of their failure to understand him. During the last week of Jesus' life Judas betrayed him; Peter denied him; the other disciples ran away and left him. None of the disciples are mentioned at the crucifixion or at his tomb and Mark does not record that Jesus met them after his Resurrection.

It is not only the failure of the disciples that is highlighted in Mark's Gospel. The religious leaders failed to accept that Jesus was the Messiah and plotted to kill him. The people of Nazareth rejected him. The Sanhedrin condemned Jesus to death and he was mocked by the ordinary people when he was dying on the cross.

• Suffering

All of the Gospels give an account of Jesus' last days but Mark's Gospel seems to particularly focus on the suffering and death of Jesus. Mark does not record the Resurrection of Jesus, although he does mention the empty tomb. Jesus is presented as the Messiah who must suffer and die before he rises again to establish the Kingdom of God on earth. Jesus also expected his followers to suffer (see Mark 8:34).

• The Messianic Secret

This is one of the most prominent themes of the Gospel. Mark presents Jesus as a secretive and mysterious figure. He teaches his disciples in secret and he orders those he has healed not to tell anyone. He commands demons to be quiet when they begin to announce his identity, and his disciples fail to understand who he really is.

Mark may have used the idea of the Messianic Secret to explain how the Messiah must suffer and die. This was not what the vast majority of Jesus' followers expected. In Mark, Jesus' disciples witness his miracles and listen to his teaching and identify him as the Messiah, but they did not expect him to be put to death at a young age.

FOR YOUR FOLDER

1. Do you think that Mark's Gospel was written at a time of persecution of Christians?

2. What evidence is there that Mark's Gospel contains eye-witness accounts?

3. Describe two characteristics of Mark's Gospel.

FURTHER THINKING

Did you know that each of the Gospel writers has his own symbol? Mark's symbol is a lion. This may be because his Gospel begins with John the Baptist crying out in the desert, like a roaring lion. Matthew's symbol is a man, Luke's is a calf and John's is an eagle.
Find out how these other symbols came about.

The Structure of Mark's Gospel

Mark's Gospel is 16 chapters long. It can be divided in the following way which helps the reader to understand what was important to Mark:

REFERENCE	CONTENT
1:1-8	John the Baptist prepares the way for Jesus
1:9-11	God identifies Jesus as the Messiah at Jesus' baptism and at the Transfiguration
1:12-13	The Temptation of Jesus before the beginning of his ministry
9:1-8	God identifies Jesus as the Messiah at the Transfiguration
1:14-13:37	The teaching and deeds of Jesus
14:1-16:20	The suffering, death, burial and Resurrection of Jesus

Before we look at the important events in the life of Jesus it will be useful to find out as much as possible about the place and time in which he lived. Background information that helps us to understand those events includes the geographical, political, social and religious background of Palestine at the time of Jesus.

PALESTINE AT THE TIME OF JESUS

Geographical Context

Jesus lived in a place called Palestine. Today this land is occupied by the countries of Israel and Palestine. It is an extremely important place for Jews, Christians and Muslims, for whom it has deep, sacred significance.

Palestine in the First Century

○ Region ruled by Archelaus (later ruled by Roman governors)

○ Region ruled by Herod Antipas

○ Region ruled by Philip

PHOENICIA
Mt Hermon
Tyre
Caesarea Philippi
ITUREA
GALILEE
Ptolemais
Capernaum
Bethsaida
Lake Galilee
Tiberias
Cana
Nazareth
Nain
Gadara
Mediterranean Sea
Caesarea
DECAPOLIS
SAMARIA
Sebaste (Samaria)
Gerasa
Joppa
PEREA
Jericho
Jerusalem
Bethany
Bethlehem
Judean Desert
Dead Sea
JUDEA
Masada
IDUMEA
NABATAEA

> **TIP**
> As you work your way through this book and come across the names of different places it is a good idea to look back to this map to see exactly where the places were.

Key Places in Palestine for a study of the life and ministry of Jesus

The River Jordan

The Jordan River runs from the uplands of Galilee into the Sea of Galilee, then through the Rift Valley and into the Dead Sea. It splits Palestine down the middle.

The Sea of Galilee

The northern area around **Galilee** is where Jesus spent much of his life. The Sea of Galilee is really a large lake 13 miles long and 7 miles across.

Galilee, Samaria and Judea

Find the **River Jordan** on the map. If you look to the left of it you will see three main regions – **Galilee** at the top, **Samaria** in the middle and **Judea** underneath. It is mainly within these regions that the ministry of Jesus took place, although he does travel beyond them. You may also recognise the place names of some of the towns, where important events happened in the life of Jesus, such as the town of Bethlehem and the city of Jerusalem.

The Wilderness of Judea

To the east of the uplands of Judea lies the Wilderness of Judea, a desolate area where John the Baptist lived and where Jesus was tempted.

A scale model of Jerusalem at the time of Jesus.

Jerusalem

Jerusalem was the capital city of Palestine. At the time of Jesus it had a population of about 50,000 people. It was a busy place, with narrow, overcrowded streets and it was part of the main corridor running between Asia and Africa. It had many visitors and the streets were full of traders and travellers, many of whom were Jews who went to visit Jerusalem to carry out their religious duties at festival times.

FURTHER THINKING

Have you ever visited Jerusalem? Do you know what it is like today? Find out 5 facts about the city of Jerusalem.

FOR YOUR FOLDER

Various events in Jesus' life took place in and around Galilee. Referring to the map on page 9, look up the following references and complete the table, writing a sentence on each of them:

Mark reference	Place	Event in Jesus' life
Mark 1:5	_____	_____
Mark 8:27	_____	_____
Mark 4:1	_____	_____
Mark 7:24	_____	_____
Mark 14:32	_____	_____
Mark 15:22	_____	_____
Mark 15:42	_____	_____

HISTORICAL AND POLITICAL CONTEXT

Palestine was a popular target for invading nations. Its central geographical position made it an important trade route and useful military base. As a result it had been governed by a number of different rulers and influenced by different cultures. For example, from 333 BC to 63 BC is known as 'the Greek Period' when many Greek customs were introduced to Palestine. This explains why the New Testament was originally written in Greek.

In 63 BC Palestine came under the control of the Romans after General Pompey captured Jerusalem. At the time of Jesus' birth, around 4 BC, the Emperor of the Roman Empire was **Caesar Augustus**. Palestine was governed by **Herod the Great** (37–4 BC).

Herod was an extremely unpopular ruler for a number of reasons:

- He was not a member of the royal family.
- He was only half-Jewish and many Jewish people disliked him because he did not take Judaism seriously.
- He interfered with religious matters. For example, he reduced the power of the **Sanhedrin**, the highest Jewish council. He also reserved the right to appoint or get rid of the **High Priest**.
- He always did as he was told by the Romans and was regarded as a 'puppet-king' and not the true ruler of the Jewish people.

- Herod had a reputation for great cruelty and had ordered the murder of several of his wives and sons. When the army objected to his actions he had 300 soldiers beaten to death.

When Herod died in 4 BC the Jews wanted the Emperor Augustus to end the Herodian rule of Palestine but the Emperor refused and the kingdom was divided between three of Herod's sons:

- Herod Antipas who took charge of **Galilee** and Perea;
- Herod Archelaus who took charge of **Judea and Samaria**; and
- Philip the Tetrarch who took charge of Iturea and Trachonitis. (The map on page 9 shows these territories.)

Out of the three, Archelaus was a brutal, corrupt and incompetent leader. In AD6 the Romans replaced him with a government official known as a procurator. The procurator answered directly to Rome and was responsible for collecting taxes, keeping the peace and administering justice, which included the power to pass the death sentence. In AD26–36 the procurator was called Pontius Pilate.

The Roman Army

The Roman army was an extremely well organised force. It was highly disciplined, strong, and feared throughout the Roman Empire. As Palestine was occupied by the Romans it was common to see Roman soldiers stationed throughout the country. The soldiers had two main duties to carry out:

- To crush any sign of rebellion against the rule of the Romans
- To make sure that taxes were collected properly

The attitude of the Jews to the Romans varied. Some looked to the benefits that were brought to Palestine, such as good roads, water and sewage systems and magnificent buildings. They also admired the strict system of law and order. Some of these Jews admired the Romans so much that they were prepared to work for them, for example, the Sadducees and the tax collectors.

The majority of the Jewish people despised the presence of the Romans in Palestine and regarded them as bullies, and outsiders in their land. Some Jews (for example, the Zealots) showed their contempt for the Romans through violence and acts of aggression.

The Sanhedrin

The Sanhedrin was the highest Jewish Council in Palestine. There were 71 members made up of religious leaders called Pharisees and Sadducees. It had some power, although it was limited. For example, the Sanhedrin did not have the power to pass the death sentence. The chairman or leader of the Sanhedrin was the High Priest.

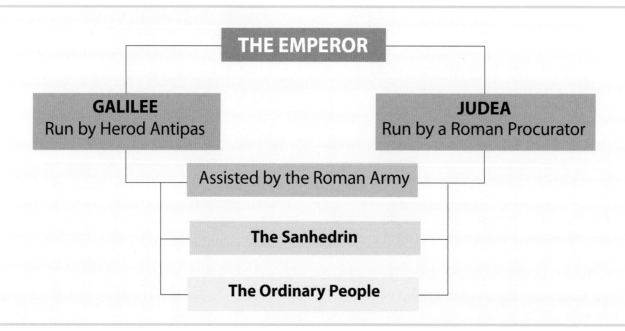

THE EMPEROR

GALILEE
Run by Herod Antipas

JUDEA
Run by a Roman Procurator

Assisted by the Roman Army

The Sanhedrin

The Ordinary People

Tax collectors

Palestine was taxed by the Romans. Local Jewish people worked as tax collectors, gathering money for the Roman government. These people were hated and considered 'sinners' because of what they did:

- They worked for the Roman government, the occupying force in Palestine and therefore were regarded as traitors.
- They had a reputation for being dishonest. It was perfectly normal for tax collectors to charge people a larger amount than was required by the Romans, so they could take a large profit themselves.
- They were not able to give money to charity because it was regarded as 'unclean'.

FOR YOUR FOLDER

1. When did Palestine become part of the Roman Empire?
2. What Emperor ruled the Roman Empire during Jesus' lifetime?
3. Who ruled Palestine at the time of Jesus' birth?
4. How was the Kingdom divided after Herod's death?
5. Explain the attitude the Jews had towards the Romans.
6. Describe some of the duties of the Roman army.
7. Why were tax-collectors not popular people?

RELIGIOUS AND SOCIAL BACKGROUND

The main religion in Palestine at the time of Jesus was **Judaism**. Judaism is one of the oldest monotheistic religions in the world ('monotheism' is the belief that there is only one God).

Covenant

Mark often refers to the Jewish concept of *covenant*. A covenant is an agreement, promise or contract. In the Jewish scriptures there are three covenants that God made with his people:

- **The Covenant with Noah**.
  You may know the story of Noah and the flood. He built an Ark and was saved from the flood along with his family and two of every kind of creature. God promised that the world would never be destroyed by flood. The sign of this covenant is the rainbow.

- **The Covenant with Abraham**.
  God made an agreement or covenant with Abraham that he would bless him and make his family a great nation. In response Abraham worshipped and obeyed God.

  The Jews believe that they were chosen from out of all the nations. The sign of this covenant is circumcision. All Jewish boys are circumcised when they are eight days old.

- **The Covenant with Moses.** God gave Moses the Ten Commandments on Mount Sinai for the people to live by.

Mark explains that Jesus brings a **New Covenant**. Like the earlier covenants, the New Covenant had a sign – the death of Jesus. Unlike the earlier covenants the New Covenant is open to everyone – not just the Jews. This radical new teaching would prove very unpopular with some people.

The Jewish Law

The first five books of the Jewish scriptures contain the Jewish Law or 'Torah', which was given by God to Moses on Mount Sinai. The Jews' ancestors had promised to keep the Law in return for being God's chosen people. Over a thousand years later, at the time of Jesus, the Law was still extremely important to the Jews.

The Jewish religious leaders who interpreted the Law were called the **Scribes**. In the Gospels they are often called the 'teachers of the Law'. People had great respect for them and would stand up in respect if a Scribe passed by. A lot of discussion took place between the Scribes over the meaning of the Law. The interpretation of the Law that they agreed upon was called the **Oral Law**. This was a list of complex rules and regulations meant to help people keep the Ten Commandments.

The Sabbath

The word 'sabbath' comes from the Hebrew word *shabat* which means 'to cease'. The Sabbath was a day of rest which began at sunset on Friday evening and lasted until sunset on Saturday evening. All work stopped on the Sabbath day.

Gentiles

A Gentile is anyone who is not Jewish. Many of them worshipped lots of different gods. Some Gentiles were known as 'God-fearers'.
They may have followed some Jewish laws or beliefs, but they were not full Jews.

Women

Women had very different lifestyles in first century Palestine compared to women in our society today. Women were second-class citizens and were regarded as inferior to men. Women were viewed as property, first of their father, then of their husband. Girls were not educated like boys. They were usually only trained in household chores like weaving and cooking.

It was considered shameful for a woman to be seen talking to any man apart from her family. Jesus challenges people's attitudes by talking freely with women, treating them with kindness and respect.

FOR YOUR FOLDER

1. What was the main religion of Palestine at the time of Jesus?

2. What is meant by the term 'monotheism'?

3. What is a covenant? Explain, using examples from the Bible.

4. What is a Gentile?

5. Look up the following references and explain what they tell us about the Sabbath:

   Genesis 2:2

   Exodus 20:11

   Numbers 15:32–36

6. Describe the place of women in Jewish society at the time of Jesus.

Plan of a synagogue.

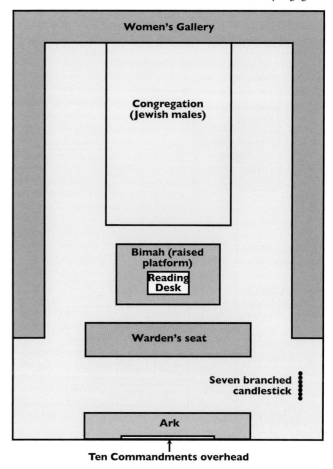

The Synagogue

A synagogue is a place of worship for Jews. The word 'synagogue' comes from a Greek word meaning 'gathering of people' or 'bringing together'. In Palestine at the time of Jesus there were synagogues in every town that had at least ten Jewish men. As well as being a house of prayer, a synagogue was a place of teaching where the scriptures were read and explained. Synagogue services were led and organised by elders. Any Jewish male could be invited to give the sermon, for example, Jesus was often asked to speak in a service (Mark 1:39). God-fearing Gentiles also attended synagogue worship.

The Temple

The first 'temple' to God was a moveable tent called the *Tabernacle*. As the people were wandering in the desert, the temple would go with them (Exodus Chapters 25–27). When the people settled, a permanent Temple was built in Jerusalem by King Solomon. Solomon's temple was later destroyed in a time of war.

At the time of Jesus, Herod the Great was building a new Temple on the original site. It was completely destroyed by the Romans in AD70. All that remains of it now is the western wall, known as the 'Wailing Wall'.

Jews praying at the 'Wailing Wall'.

The ruins of the Kfar Bar'am synagogue in upper Galilee.

15

The Temple was important because it was the only place where the Jews could offer sacrifices to God. Sacrifices were made by a priest on the Altar of sacrifice (see diagram).

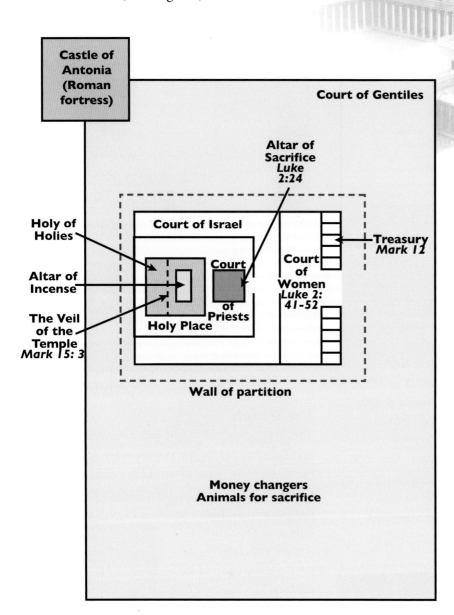

The Temple was spacious and contained one outer court and four enclosed courts:

• **The Outer Court: The Court of Gentiles**
This courtyard was inside the wall of the Temple and was the only part of the Temple grounds that a Gentile (non-Jew) was allowed to enter. Temple markets were held here which catered for worshippers' activities. Money-changers

provided suitable coins for the Temple offering: coins with Caesar's head were not allowed. Animals for sacrifice were sold at the Temple markets as they had already been checked for purity by the Temple inspectors.

It was in the Court of the Gentiles that Jesus overturned the tables of the money changers (Mark 11:15–19 – see page 64).

• **The Court of Women**

Jewish women were allowed to enter this court but were not allowed to go beyond it. The Temple treasury for offerings of money was kept there.

It was here that Jesus and the disciples observed the widow give her offering (see page 66).

• **The Court of Israel**

This court encircled three sides of the Holy Place. Jewish men were allowed into this court. It was a place where men and priests came to pray.

• **The Holy Place**

The Holy Place was where the Priests could go to burn incense. It was divided into two by a thick curtain called 'The Veil'. Once a year, on the Day of Atonement, the High Priest went beyond the Veil into the Holy of Holies. The Holy of Holies was thought of as the place where God was most present.

FOR YOUR FOLDER

1. What was the synagogue used for apart from religious services?

2. Explain how the Temple was different to the synagogue.

3. List the different courts of the Temple and explain who was allowed to enter each court.

4. What was the altar used for?

5. When was the Temple destroyed?

RELIGIOUS GROUPS WITHIN JUDAISM

The Pharisees

As you learn about the life and ministry of Jesus you will hear a lot about his relationship with the Pharisees and how they opposed Jesus on many occasions. They were the largest and most influential of the religious groups within Judaism in the first century. They lived strictly by the **Oral Law** and were often criticised by Jesus because of this. Jesus believed that many of them did not have genuine faith but were obsessed with keeping petty laws. He often called them hypocrites.

The word *Pharisee* means 'separated one'. They aimed to separate themselves from anything that they believed would make them 'unclean'. This included Romans, Gentiles, and any other Jews who had become 'unclean'.

The Pharisees had a strong belief that a Messiah, or saviour, would come from God to deliver the Jews from their hardships, leading them into a time of religious and political good fortune. They also believed in life after death and bodily resurrection.

The Sadducees

These were a small group of wealthy, upper class religious leaders who looked down on the ordinary people. Most of them were priests. They tried to be friendly with the Romans to keep the power that they held. They opposed any ideas that threatened their privileged position, for example, the expectation of a Messiah. They differed from the Pharisees in that they did not accept the **Oral Law** or the idea of a bodily resurrection after death. However, the Sadducees joined with the Pharisees against Jesus because he criticised them and they saw him as a threat to their relationship with the Romans.

The High Priest

The religious leader of the Jews was the High Priest. He was in charge of the Sanhedrin, the highest Jewish council. Caiaphas was the High Priest at the time of Jesus' death.

The Zealots

The Zealots were a group of Jews who used terrorist tactics against the Romans to gain their religious and political freedom. They were passionate about their beliefs and felt strongly that they should have a land of their own. The Zealots refused to pay taxes and used violence against the Romans.

The Romans refused to tolerate this kind of rebellion and on several occasions they tried to destroy the Zealots. In AD66 the Zealots led a rebellion against the Romans which ended in AD73 when the fortress at Masada was attacked by the Romans. Those inside killed themselves rather than be captured by the Romans. Simon, one of Jesus' disciples, was a Zealot.

The mountain-top fortress at Masada. The Romans could only reach the fortress by building a huge ramp.

The Samaritans

Samaria lay between Galilee and Judea. The people who lived there, the Samaritans, were a mixed race. They were descended from Jews who had intermarried with other races when the Assyrians invaded Israel in the eighth century BC, and so they were only partly Jewish.

The Samaritans worshipped the same God as the Jews and accepted some of their Law. The Gospels show us that there was intense hatred between the Jews and the Samaritans (Luke 19:25–37).

Chapter 2

THE IDENTITY OF JESUS

In this section we will be looking at different events in the life of Jesus that give us some insight into who Jesus claimed to be and what people in first century Palestine thought about him.

TITLES OF JESUS

Throughout the Gospel, Mark uses a number of different 'titles' when referring to Jesus. Each tells us something different about the identity of Jesus.

TIP
As you study the Gospel, make a note of the passages where each of these titles is used. It will be useful to give examples in examination.

Son of God

In the Jewish Scriptures the king of Israel was sometimes called God's son (Psalm 2:7) but Jesus never used this title to describe himself. Mark uses the title 'Son of God' at Jesus' baptism (Mark 1:1–13), and his Transfiguration (Mark 9:2–13). The title 'Son of God' became a more popular way to describe Jesus after his death and Resurrection, and is used widely in the Church today.

Christ – Messiah

The Greek word *christ*, and the Hebrew word *messiah*, both mean 'anointed one'. In the Jewish scriptures the word was used for people who were set aside to carry out a special task. High priests and kings were anointed with oil as a sign that God had chosen them.

The Jews believed that a Messiah would come to save them. Some Jews expected the Messiah to be a prophet, like Moses. Others expected a military Messiah who would drive out the Romans and set up a kingdom on Earth for them, restoring the glory of the reign of King David.

Jesus never referred to himself as 'Messiah'. Rather than a powerful military leader, Jesus seems to identify himself with Isaiah's prophecy of a 'suffering servant' (Isaiah 52:13–53:12). When the disciple Peter described Jesus as the Messiah (Mark 8:27-33), he accepted it, but warned the disciples to tell no one.

At various points in his Gospel, Mark makes it very clear to the reader that Jesus is the Messiah. Examples include: Jesus' baptism (Mark 1:9-13); Jesus' entry into Jerusalem (Mark 11:1-11); and the trial before the Sanhedrin (Mark 14:53-65).

Son of David

King David (1 & 2 Samuel, 1 Kings, 1 Chronicles) was regarded as the greatest king of Israel. During his reign Israel was successful and had its own empire. Most Jews expected that their future Messiah would be a descendant of King David, chosen by God to rule as king. Matthew and Luke, the Gospel writers, trace Jesus' family tree back to David. When people used this title for Jesus in the Gospel stories it shows that they believed him to be the Messiah, for example, the healing of the blind man (Mark 10:46-52).

Son of Man

Jesus often referred to himself using the title 'Son of Man'. This had two meanings:

Firstly, this title was used by the prophet Ezekiel to describe himself. He wanted to show that he was an ordinary person. Likewise, Jesus may have called himself 'Son of Man' to remind his disciples that he was a person like them.

Secondly, 'Son of Man' is used in the prophecy of Daniel 7:13 to describe a figure with authority from God. Many people connected this prophecy with the idea of the coming Messiah.

Jesus used the title 'Son of Man' when he talked about his ministry on earth, when he was talking about his death, and when he spoke about his Ascension into heaven.

Saviour

The name 'Jesus' means 'God saves'. The Jews expected a military Messiah who would overthrow their enemies. However, Jesus as Saviour means something else for Christians. Christians believe that Jesus offers salvation to humankind (saves them) through his death and Resurrection. This means that Jesus sacrificed himself and took the punishment that was due to humankind.

FOR YOUR FOLDER

Which of the titles given to Jesus do you think would appeal most to people today? Give reasons for your answer.

THE MINISTRY OF JOHN THE BAPTIST
MARK 1:1-13

Mark's Gospel opens with a declaration about Jesus' identity:

> "This is the good news about Jesus Christ, the Son of God" (1:1)

There is an immediate connection made with the prophecies of Jewish Scripture (Isaiah 40:3). The prophecy talks about a messenger that God will send to prepare the way for the coming of the promised Messiah.

In Mark's Gospel this messenger is John the Baptist who appeared in the desert of Judea. John's role was to prepare the people for the coming of the Messiah. Mark describes how John does this by telling people to turn away from their sins and be baptised. John's preaching was so successful that many people gathered at the River Jordan to be baptised.

Baptism was not a new idea. Being ritually and symbolically cleansed by total immersion in water is a Jewish ritual. John baptised people as a sign of repentance - a way of saying sorry to God and making a fresh start in life.

Mark describes John the Baptist like an ancient Jewish prophet. We usually imagine a prophet to be someone who makes predictions about the future. However, in the Bible a prophet is a person who explained the implications of God's word for the present day.

Mark believed that John was just like the prophet Elijah, that he was a second Elijah. We can see this from the words of Jesus in Mark 9:12-13:

"I tell you, however, that Elijah has already come and the people treated him just as they pleased, as the Scriptures say about him."

Another clue that John was a second Elijah was the way he looked. He dressed almost exactly like Elijah:

"'He was wearing a cloak made of animal skins, tied with a leather belt', they answered. 'It's Elijah!' the king exclaimed."
(2 Kings 1:8)

"John wore clothes made of camel's hair, with a belt round his waist, and his food was locusts and wild honey."
(Mark 1:6)

John explained to the crowds gathered at the River Jordan that his baptism was not enough for salvation. He was only preparing them for what was yet to come:

"The man who will come after me is much greater than I am. I am not good enough even to bend down and untie his sandals. I baptise with water, but he will baptise you with the Holy Spirit"'(1:8).

The baptism of Jesus by John the Baptist is recorded in all four Gospels. Mark's account is quite brief which gives a sense of urgency to events.

It is one of two incidents that shows that Jesus was God's Son. The Transfiguration is the other (see page 23).

Mark records that when John baptised Jesus, the baptism was accompanied by three important events, which were signs of God's presence:

1. The heavens opened. Only Jesus saw this, which has led some scholars to suggest that this was a vision given to Jesus, rather than an actual event.

2. The Spirit of God came upon Jesus like a dove. In the Jewish Scriptures the dove was regarded as the bringer of good news (for example, in the story of Noah – Genesis 8:8–12). It came to mean a sign of peace.

3. A voice from heaven spoke, quoting Psalm 2:7 and Isaiah 42:1, confirming Jesus' divine identity. Jesus was chosen and appointed by God to do his work.

Through the power of the Holy Spirit Jesus was equipped to carry out his ministry.

IN A GROUP

Today it is through the rite of baptism that people become members of the Christian Church. In the New Testament it was mainly adults that were baptised. As time went on the practice of including children in the blessings of baptism became popular.

Discuss the differences between adult and infant baptism. Do you think people should be baptised as adults or as infants?

FOR YOUR FOLDER

1. Copy and complete the table below which lists the times and places where Jesus was called 'God's Son' in Mark's Gospel.

Reference	Who calls Jesus 'God's Son'?
1:1	
1:11	
3:11	
5:5-7	
9:7	
13:32	
14:61	
15:39	

2. How could John the Baptist be compared to the prophet Elijah?

3. What three important events happened as Jesus was baptised?

4. Why do you think Jesus was baptised?

5. Do you think it is necessary for Christians to be baptised?

6. 'Through his baptism Jesus showed true humility. Christians should follow his example.' How do you think Christians could do this in their everyday lives?

PETER'S DECLARATION ABOUT JESUS
MARK 8:27–33

An important event took place at Caesarea Philippi which revealed Jesus as the promised Messiah. Jesus openly asked his disciples about his identity. His first question, *"Who do people say I am?"* shows us what the general Jewish public thought: that the Son of Man was John the Baptist, Elijah, Jeremiah or some other prophet.

Caesarea Philippi

Jesus' second question was directed at his disciples: *"Who do you say I am?"* Peter, who was one of Jesus' closest disciples, was very clear about his opinion: *"You are the Messiah."*

This is the first time the term 'messiah' is used by Mark since his introduction in chapter one. It shows that Peter was one of the first disciples to truly understand who Jesus was. Peter later becomes one of the key leaders of the early Church.

Jesus then ordered the disciples not to tell anyone about what had happened. This is an example of the Messianic Secret (see page 7).

Jesus then spoke to the disciples for the first time of his forthcoming suffering, death and Resurrection. Although Peter had just revealed that Jesus was the Messiah, Jesus referred to himself as the 'Son of Man' (it is interesting that Jesus is the only person in Mark's Gospel who uses this term).

Peter must have been horrified at the suggestion that the Messiah must suffer, for he took Jesus to one side and rebuked him. Like many other Jews, Peter probably thought that the Messiah would be like a victorious king who would save Israel from the Romans, not someone who would suffer a humiliating death. Jesus was clearly angry with

Peter for trying to stand in the way of God's plans for he called him 'Satan'.

This event marks a turning-point in the story – events move quickly from this moment on towards the last events in Jesus' life.

1. Explain the meaning of the title 'Messiah'.
2. Give an account of Peter's declaration about Jesus.
3. Why do you think it was Peter who answered Jesus' question at Caesarea Philippi?
4. Explain why Jesus was angry with Peter.

THE TRANSFIGURATION
MARK 9:2–13

Six days after Peter confessed that Jesus was *"the Messiah, the Son of the Living God"*, a dramatic event called the Transfiguration took place. There are three important things to note:

1. **The change in Jesus' appearance:**
   The word **transfigured** means to be transformed or to change appearance, making something more spiritual or important. At the Transfiguration, Jesus' appearance was changed by becoming *"shining white"* (9:3).

2. **The presence of Moses and Elijah:**
   Jesus was shown to be equal to the two most important figures in Judaism: Moses and Elijah.

   Moses represented the **Law**
   Elijah represented the **Prophets**

The Law and the Prophets are the foundation of Jewish religion. The appearance of Moses and Elijah communicates that Jesus fulfilled their prophecies, and his teaching fulfilled the Law.

It was believed that figures from the scriptures would appear in the lead up to the end of the world.

IN A GROUP

Discuss:

Why is it important for Christians that Jesus was identified as the Messiah, and not just a good man?

FURTHER THINKING

Carry out a survey among your family and friends about who people think Jesus was. Present your findings in a bar-graph or a pie-chart. Try to include the opinions of people from a variety of ages.

warned the disciples not to tell anyone about the Transfiguration until the Son of Man had risen from the dead. This is another example of the Messianic Secret. There would come a time, after his death, when the significance of the transfiguration would be understood.

The disciples were confused about what Jesus meant when he said he would rise from the dead. How could the magnificent, transfigured Jesus they had just seen be linked to suffering and death?

They began to ask Jesus questions about the Jewish prophecies of a coming Messiah. They refer specifically to Malachi 3:1 and 4:5-6 when they ask: *"Why do the teachers of the Law say that Elijah has to come first?"* It was believed that Elijah would return, to turn the hearts of the people back to God before the Messiah appeared (Malachi 4:5-6).

The disciples were afraid of what was going on. Peter suggested marking the place where the Transfiguration had taken place by building three tents for Jesus, Moses and Elijah. This was a Jewish custom to remember the great figures of Judaism. Jews today still celebrate the 'Feast of Tabernacles'.

Jesus told his disciples that Elijah had already come. Mark 9:12–13 tells us that he was referring to John the Baptist– remember that John and Elijah both dressed and acted in similar ways. Slowly the disciples were beginning to understand more about Jesus.

A Jewish shelter during the Feast of Tabernacles

3. The cloud and the voice:

A shining cloud also came from above and a voice spoke from the cloud, confirming that Jesus was the Son of God. In Jewish scripture a cloud was a symbol of God's presence (Exodus 24:15–18; 40:34). The words spoken were similar to those at Jesus' baptism (see page 21).

These words left the disciples in no doubt that Jesus was in fact God's Son. At that point the figures of Moses and Elijah had disappeared. Jesus

FOR YOUR FOLDER

1. What does the word Transfiguration mean?
2. Where did the Transfiguration take place?
3. Who was with Jesus at the Transfiguration?
4. Name the figures from Jewish Scripture who appeared with Jesus at the Transfiguration and explain their significance.
5. Name another occasion when God said he was pleased with Jesus.
6. Why do you think the Transfiguration was important for the disciples?

JESUS' ENTRY INTO JERUSALEM
MARK 11:1–11

Throughout Jesus' ministry he cautioned his followers many times not to tell anyone about miracles he performed and it seemed he wanted to keep his true identity as Messiah a secret. Now that had changed. Rather than avoiding attention, Jesus made a grand entrance into the city.

Jesus was confirming his true identity as:

- **a popular figure** – Jesus was popular with the ordinary people. They did not regard him as a hypocrite, like other religious leaders.

- **a humble servant** – Jesus rode on a colt (a young male donkey), not a horse as a king would have done. Jesus was entering Jerusalem as a servant.

- **the 'Son of David'**– the Messiah predicted in the Jewish scriptures.

- **'Lord'** (11:3) – This is the only place in Mark's Gospel where Jesus used the title 'Lord' of himself.

Jesus deliberately fulfilled Zechariah's prophecy:

"Tell the city of Zion, Look, your king is coming to you! He is humble and rides on a donkey and on a colt, the foal of a donkey" (Zechariah 21:5) .

Zion was a poetic name for Jerusalem and the Jews believed that Jerusalem belonged to the Messiah.

The crowds showed that they believed Jesus was the Messiah by spreading their clothes on the road and throwing palm branches before him. They sang words of praise which come from Psalm 118:25–26. *'Hosanna'* means 'save now!', but it was commonly used as a word of praise. It was an amazing scene of great celebration.

FOR YOUR FOLDER

1. What title did the crowds use for Jesus as he entered Jerusalem?

2. Explain why Jesus rode on a donkey and not a horse.

3. Whose prophecy did Jesus fulfil?

4. Jesus entered Jerusalem on a donkey, symbolising peace, rather than the military power of a horse. How do you think Christians could follow Jesus' example in their lives today?

THE CALMING OF THE STORM

MARK 4:35–41

This story is an example of the power Jesus had over nature. It was believed that God could control the weather. In the Jewish Scriptures God is described as having power over the sea (Psalm 89; Psalm 93:3–4; Psalm 107:23–30 and Isaiah 51:9–10). The detail in description of this event suggests that it was an eye-witness account.

It was evening time and Jesus and his disciples had taken a boat on to the Sea of Galilee to get a break from the crowds that had gathered to hear Jesus teaching. Sudden storms are common on the Sea of Galilee so it would not have been too much of a shock for them to get caught up in one. However, the storm described here must have been particularly severe– some of the disciples were experienced fishermen and they were terrified.

Jesus was asleep with his head on a pillow. Sleeping peacefully was a sign that a person had complete trust in God (Proverbs 3:23-24; Job 11:18-19). This contrasts with the lack of faith shown by the disciples. Their distress is clearly seen in the fact that they thought Jesus was sleeping because he did not care about what was happening. They were wrong. Jesus stood up and commanded the wind to *"be quiet"* and the waves to *"be still"*.

This miracle showed the disciples that Jesus was no ordinary man, but the Son of God. They asked each other, *"Who is this man? Even the winds and waves obey him!"(4:41).*

THE MEANING OF THE STORY

The story would have given comfort to many of the first readers of Mark's Gospel. They were suffering fierce persecution from the Roman Emperor Nero. He was notoriously cruel in his treatment of the Christians. The disciple Peter is said to have died in Nero's persecution.

Some scholars have suggested that the story can be interpreted as an allegory. The boat is the Christian Church and the storm is the persecution that it faced. Christians are assured that Christ is in control but they must have faith.

The story of the calming of the storm is still important to Christians today who believe that it gives them assurance that they can rely on God in times of trouble and uncertainty.

FOR YOUR FOLDER

1. How could this event be described as a 'nature miracle'?

2. How did Jesus calm the storm?

3. What does this miracle teach about faith?

4. Why do you think the disciples asked, *"Who is this man?"*

5. Explain the significance of this story for Mark's first readers.

THE REQUEST OF JAMES AND JOHN
MARK 10:35–45

The rest of the disciples were angry with James and John when they heard about the conversation. So Jesus spoke to them all about the true meaning of discipleship:

> *"If one of you wants to be great, he must be the servant of the rest, and if one of you wants to be first, he must be the slave of all." (10:43–44)*

Jesus showed them that the Son of Man was to be a servant of all people. He urged them to follow his example.

Peter, James and John formed the inner circle of the disciples. On this occasion James and John asked Jesus if they could have the best seats in heaven, one to sit on Jesus' right and the other on Jesus' left. Jesus explained to them that they did not understand what they were asking for, because such a request would also involve sharing in his suffering.

James and John insisted that they could endure the same 'cup of suffering' as Jesus and be baptised in the same way. Jesus was referring to his death, but it is obvious that James and John did not realise what Jesus was talking about. Jesus added that God alone will decide who sits where in his Kingdom.

FOR YOUR FOLDER

1. What request did James and John have?
2. What did Jesus stress that they should be prepared to do?
3. What did Jesus mean when he said, *"If one of you wants to be great, he must be the servant of the rest"*?
4. What can Christians learn about discipleship from this story?

FURTHER THINKING

For some Christians, following Jesus has meant facing death.

Later in the book of Acts we learn how James was put to death for being a follower of Christ (Acts 12:2). Over the centuries, many people have been killed for their faith or 'martyred'.

Find out what you can about the stories of famous Christian martyrs.

NOTE

CUP OF SUFFERING
In the Jewish Scriptures the image of a cup was used as a symbol of both suffering and joy. Jesus also uses this term in the Garden of Gethsemane (14:36).

BLIND BARTIMAEUS

MARK 10:46–52

The last miracle recorded in Mark's Gospel tells of the healing of a blind man. It takes place just before the last week of Jesus' life.

Jesus was leaving Jericho, followed by a large crowd, on his way to Jerusalem when he came across a blind beggar called Bartimaeus. The crowd was probably on the way to Jerusalem for the Passover festival.

Bartimaeus called out, *"Jesus! Son of David! Take pity on me!" (10:47)*. It is significant that Bartimaeus addressed Jesus in this way. It shows that he believed that Jesus was the Messiah. The crowd told him to be quiet but he refused. He was determined to meet Jesus.

Jesus took notice of his persistence and called for him to come over. At this point, Jesus was no longer concerned with keeping his identity as Messiah a secret, and he asked the man what he wanted. Bartimaeus told Jesus he wanted to see again and Jesus told him: *"Your faith has made you well"(10:52)*. The Greek words that Mark uses can also mean *"Your faith has saved you."*

Bartimaeus immediately followed Jesus on the road, which suggests that he became a part of Jesus' group of followers. The road they were on led to Jerusalem, which was where Jesus would meet his death.

Some people believe that, through this story, Mark was urging his readers to become believers. A parallel can be drawn between the physical blindness of Bartimaeus and the spiritual blindness of the disciples which was described in the story of the request of James and John.

FOR YOUR FOLDER

1. Where was Jesus going when he met Bartimaeus?

2. What did Bartimaeus shout out to Jesus?

3. How did Bartimaeus show that he was persistent?

4. What is the significance of the term 'Son of David'?

5. How did the faith of Bartimaeus contrast with that of the disciples?

6. Why do some people think that Bartimaeus became a follower of Jesus?

7. 'True faith is often found where you least expect it'. Do you agree or disagree? Give reasons for your answer.

Chapter 3

JESUS THE MIRACLE WORKER

Jesus' miracles have been a topic for debate for many people. The key questions that people ask are:

"Were they actual supernatural events?"

"Did they just seem to be miraculous when, in reality, they had a logical and scientific explanation?"

Mark was writing at a time when many people believed in the power of miracles. He did not try to explain the miracles by giving a detailed scientific account of them. His aim was not to prove that a particular event was a miracle but to show the amazing way in which God worked through Jesus.

A MAN WITH AN EVIL SPIRIT   MARK 1:21–28

The first miracle recorded by Mark happens in the town of Capernaum on the Sabbath and involves the casting out of an evil spirit from a man. It was commonly accepted at the time of Jesus that there were millions of evil spirits in the world. It was thought that these spirits could possess people and cause mental and physical illness.

On this occasion a man possessed with an evil spirit screamed at Jesus when he was teaching in the synagogue:

"What do you want with us, Jesus of Nazareth? Are you here to destroy us? I know who you are – you are God's holy messenger!" (1:24)

The use of the title 'God's holy messenger' shows that the evil spirit recognised that Jesus was the Messiah.

This is an example of a contest between good and evil. In this miracle Jesus showed that he had authority over evil spirits. He cast the spirit out from the man with a direct command:

"Be quiet and come out of the man!"

The man shook as the evil spirit came out of him. The people were amazed at Jesus' power. Unlike the evil spirit, they still did not recognise who Jesus was but news about Jesus spread quickly through Galilee.

Capernaum

FOR YOUR FOLDER

1. Where was Jesus when he cast out the evil spirit from the man?
2. What title did the evil spirit use when it spoke to Jesus?
3. Why do you think this miracle can be described as a contest between good and evil?
4. How did Jesus show his authority over the evil spirit?

IN A GROUP

'The Gospel writers were confusing mental illness with the possession of evil spirits.'

Do you agree or disagree? Give reasons for your answer.

JESUS HEALS MANY PEOPLE MARK 1:29–34

Immediately after Jesus cast the evil spirit out of the man, Jesus was taken to the house of Simon (probably Simon Peter). His mother-in-law was very sick with a fever, possibly flu or malaria.

Jesus took her by the hand and helped her up, and the fever left her. Immediately she began waiting on them– probably preparing food and drink. This shows the miraculous speed of the cure.

Jesus broke social conventions by helping this woman on the Sabbath. The Law stated that no work should be done on the Sabbath (Jeremiah 17:24), and that included helping the sick and needy.

After the sun had set and the Sabbath was over, the people of the town of Capernaum brought their sick friends and relatives to Jesus for healing. Jesus also cast out demons and ordered them to be silent concerning his identity as Messiah. This shows that Jesus wanted people to follow him for his teaching, and not for his ability to perform miraculous acts.

FOR YOUR FOLDER

1. Which disciple's mother-in-law was sick with a fever?

2. How did Jesus heal her?

3. Explain how she showed her appreciation for what Jesus had done.

4. What do you think Christians today can learn from her attitude?

5. Why did the people wait until sunset before they brought their sick friends and relatives to Jesus?

6. Explain why Jesus silenced the demons that recognised him.

A MAN WITH A DREADED SKIN DISEASE
MARK 1:40–45

At the time of Jesus the skin disease known as 'leprosy' was common. Strict instructions were given in the Jewish Scriptures to help prevent the spread of such diseases (see Leviticus 13:45-46). It was thought that leprosy was contagious and people with the disease were treated as social outcasts.

This is the only time in Mark's Gospel where Jesus healed out of pity. He showed great compassion to the man, not only by healing him, but by touching him. Jewish people would have been shocked at this because they believed that contact with lepers would make a person 'unclean'. Jesus was not happy with this misconception. He did not like the fact that the Law separated someone from society because they had been pronounced unclean.

The leper showed that he had great faith in Jesus' ability to heal him when he said to Jesus *"Sir, if you want to, you can make me clean" (1:40)* Afterwards Jesus advised the man to go and show himself to the priest for examination. The priest was the only one who had the authority to declare a person clean again. Jesus told the healed man not to tell anyone else about the miracle. This is another example of the Messianic Secret (see page 7). Mark records how the man could not keep the news of his cure to himself and told everyone. As a result, Jesus kept himself away from public places.

This miracle teaches Christians today that God is concerned about them and will reach out to touch them in times of need. It also reminds them that they should be willing to reach out and care for those shunned by society.

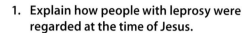

FOR YOUR FOLDER

1. Explain how people with leprosy were regarded at the time of Jesus.

2. Why was Jesus' treatment of this man out of the ordinary?

3. How did the man in this story impress Jesus?

4. How could Christians today learn from Jesus' attitude towards 'lepers'?

IN A GROUP

What groups of people are outcast from society today, as the leprosy sufferers were outcast in Jesus' day?

NOTE

The Leprosy Mission

What is Leprosy?
Leprosy is a mildly infectious disease caused by a tiny rod-like germ called *Mycobacterium leprae* which can damage the nerves under the skin. Untreated it can lead to loss of feeling in hands, feet and face. With the loss of feeling and absence of pain, injuries can occur leading to disability.

Can it be cured?
Leprosy can be cured in as little as 6 months using multi-drug therapy.

Who has Leprosy?
Leprosy can affect people of all ages and social backgrounds although 90% of all cases occur in less developed areas of the world.

How do people get Leprosy?
Leprosy is not passed on by touch, drinking dirty water, or sharing food with someone who has leprosy, nor is it hereditary. It is thought an infected person passes it on by coughing and sneezing.

What is The Leprosy Mission?
The Leprosy Mission is an international Christian charity which works in over 28 countries worldwide to provide help to those affected by leprosy.

What does The Leprosy Mission do?
The Leprosy Mission provides medical services, education scholarships, work training, low-cost housing, small business loans and business training. The Mission's aim is to restore leprosy patients' health, independence and self respect.

THE LEPROSY MISSION

A PARALYSED MAN

MARK 2:1–12

This miracle marks the beginning of conflict between Jesus and the religious leaders. Jesus was in Capernaum, probably at the house of Simon Peter and Andrew. A large crowd had gathered and Jesus was teaching them. However, he was interrupted by the arrival of four men carrying their paralysed friend.

The crowd was so large that the men could not get near Jesus so they had carried their friend up onto the roof, made a hole in it, and lowered him through the ceiling. Jesus was impressed by the faith of these men and healed their paralysed friend.

He said to the man *"My son, your sins are forgiven."* The Pharisees standing near must have been shocked because they considered his words to be blasphemy (2:7). They believed that only God could forgive sins, so in their opinion Jesus was claiming to be equal with God. Imagine their outrage.

Jesus replies to them: *"I will prove to you, then, that the Son of Man has authority on earth to forgive sins"* *(2:10).* This is the only place in Mark's Gospel where Jesus claims to have the authority to forgive sins.

Jesus told the paralysed man to pick up his mat and go home. Everyone was amazed at the miracle and praised God because they had never seen anything like it before.

FOR YOUR FOLDER

1. What did Jesus say when he saw the faith of the friends of the paralysed man?

2. Why would the Pharisees have been furious about this?

3. Explain why Jesus may have called himself 'Son of Man' on this occasion.

4. How might Christians today be influenced by Jesus' attitude to the sick?

FURTHER THINKING

Do you think it is important for Christians to believe that miracles really happen? Discuss in a small group.

A MAN WITH A PARALYSED HAND

MARK 3:1–6

Some of the Pharisees wanted to accuse Jesus of doing wrong, so they asked him if he thought it was against the Jewish Law to heal on the Sabbath. The Pharisees taught that you could give medical assistance on the Sabbath only if someone's life was in danger.

Jesus claimed the right to heal on the Sabbath to help someone in need. He healed the man, saying *"Stretch out your hand"* (3:5). Notice that on this occasion Mark makes no mention of the faith of the healed man. Having failed to trick Jesus, the Pharisees left and made plans to kill him.

could do this. This shows that not all the religious leaders were against Jesus.

Jesus followed him immediately but was side-tracked along the way by a woman who had suffered from severe bleeding for twelve years. In the eyes of the Jewish Law, her condition made her ceremonially unclean, preventing her from joining in Jewish festivals and ceremonies. She was obviously ashamed and tried to touch Jesus' cloak secretly, in the hope that this action would cure her. Clearly, like Jairus, she had great faith.

Jesus was fully aware of what was happening and praised the woman: *"My daughter, your faith has made you well" (5:34)*. Jesus' reaction to this woman was unusual in a society where men were regarded as superior. Not only did he speak to the woman, but he addressed her using a term of deep respect. He also wanted the woman to know that her faith had played a part in making her well. Faith is the key to understanding both of these miracles.

FOR YOUR FOLDER

1. What did the Pharisees believe about helping people on the Sabbath?

2. How did Jesus justify healing on the Sabbath?

3. Explain why Jesus' words and actions would have angered the Pharisees.

IN A GROUP

1. The paralysed man's condition was not life threatening and Jesus could have avoided conflict by waiting until the Sabbath was over to heal the man. Why does he not do this?

2. Do you think Christians should always try to avoid arguments or disagreements?

3. 'The Christian idea of Sunday as a day of rest is outdated in the twenty-first century.'

   Discuss whether you agree or disagree. Give reasons for your answer.

Afterwards Jesus went to Jairus' house where people had gathered in mourning, and preparations were being made for the child's funeral. The crowd laughed when Jesus claimed that the child was not dead but sleeping. Jesus insisted that they leave the room and he then took the girl's hand and she got up. The news of this miracle spread around the whole area.

JAIRUS' DAUGHTER AND A WOMAN
MARK 5:21–43

Jesus was approached by Jairus– an official from the local synagogue. He was distraught because his daughter had just died and he begged Jesus to bring her back to life. Such was Jesus' reputation as a miracle worker that the official had faith that Jesus

The healing of Jairus' daughter shows that Jesus had power over death.

JESUS FEEDS FIVE THOUSAND PEOPLE

MARK 6:30–44

The level of detail in Mark's account of this event, such as the greenness of the grass and the people sitting in rows, suggests that it is based on an eyewitness account.

Jesus took the disciples away from the crowds to rest, but the crowds followed them. Jesus was teaching the people until late, and the disciples suggested sending the people to nearby villages to get food. Jesus tells the disciples to give them something to eat. The disciples could find only five loaves and two fish.

Jesus gave thanks for the food and gave it to the disciples to pass out. All the people ate their fill and there were five baskets of food left over.

Not only does this miracle show Jesus' power, it recalls two miracles from the Jewish Scriptures.

In Exodus 16:4–15 God miraculously fed Moses and the Hebrews with manna in the wilderness. In 2 Kings 4:42–44 the prophet Elisha feeds 100 men with 20 loaves of bread. Like the events at the Transfiguration, Jesus is seen as fulfilling the two foundations of Jewish religion: the Law (Moses) and the prophets (Elisha).

This miracle also signifies that Jesus is the Messiah. One of the beliefs about the Messiah is that his reign would begin with a banquet. Mark's readers would also have been reminded of Jesus' Last Supper before his death.

Some people have suggested that there is not really a miracle in this story. They suggest that the crowds actually had food with them, and were inspired by Jesus' teaching to share with each other. This does not explain the significance of Jesus' later references to this event (Mark 8:18-21).

IN A GROUP

Discuss the following different opinions about this miracle:

"It was a real miracle. It happened exactly how Mark describes it!"

"Everybody just had their own food with them. It was like sharing your packed lunch with people. It was no miracle!"

"It was a miracle of sharing."

"There were 12 baskets of food left over. Where did they come from?"

THE SYRO-PHOENICIAN WOMAN'S DAUGHTER

MARK 7:24–30

On this occasion we get a glimpse into the attitude some people had towards both women and Gentiles. Jesus went into the territory of Tyre, in Phoenicia, which was in the Roman province of Syria (find this on the map on page 9). A woman asked Jesus to cast out an evil spirit from her daughter. News of Jesus' miracles had obviously spread to Gentile areas.

The focus of this story is on the conversation Jesus had with the woman, rather than on the miracle itself. The woman calls Jesus *'sir'*, meaning *'Lord'*, which was a title for God. Jesus seems to ignore the woman's request, which may seem a strange thing for him to do. His words to her may seem shocking or even rude:

"It isn't right to take the children's food and throw it to the dogs" (Mark 7:27).

The term 'dog' was a common description used for Gentiles. The woman's persistence is seen in her clever use of words:

"Even the dogs under the table eat the children's leftovers" (Mark 7:28).

Jesus may have been testing this woman's faith, but he was delighted with the results and commended her for her great faith. He healed her daughter and showed that the Kingdom of God is open to everyone.

Women at the time of Jesus were treated as second-class citizens. This woman would have been doubly despised by Jewish men because she was a Gentile. This did not matter to Jesus, who accepted all people equally. The key point is that the Gospel is not just for the Jews, but for everyone. This is called 'universalism'.

UNIVERSALISM is the idea that the Gospel message is for everyone, regardless of race, gender, or religion. No one person is more deserving of the Gospel than anyone else.

This would have been a difficult concept for some to accept. They were used to looking down upon women, Gentiles, and other outcasts.

FOR YOUR FOLDER

1. What opinion did the Gentile woman have of Jesus?

2. Jesus spoke to the woman about throwing the children's food to the dogs. What was he really talking about?

3. What does this miracle teach about 'universalism'?

4. What does this story teach about racism?

A BOY WITH AN EVIL SPIRIT   MARK 9:14–29

This miracle took place immediately after the Transfiguration. While Jesus had been up the mountain with Peter, James and John, the other disciples had been trying to cast an evil spirit out of a boy, without any success.

When Jesus and the three disciples came down the mountain the rest of the disciples were having an argument with the religious leaders. Mark describes that the people gathered were *"greatly surprised"* *(9:15)* when they saw Jesus. It is possible that his face was still shining after the Transfiguration, just like when Moses returned from Mount Sinai (Exodus 34:30).

The father of the boy explained to Jesus that the evil spirit would cause his son to fall on the ground, foam at the mouth, grit his teeth and then his whole body would become stiff. When asked if he would help, Jesus answers: *"Everything is possible for the person who has faith" (9:23).* The boy's father asked Jesus to help him have more faith. Jesus then commanded the spirit to come out of the boy. The crowds thought that the boy had died, but Jesus helped him to his feet.

Mark's record of this event talks a lot about faith. He highlights the failure of the disciples– they had been unable to heal the boy because of a lack of faith (9:18). Jesus was obviously disappointed in them (9:19). They had been given the power to heal by Jesus (3:15) but it seemed they still hadn't enough faith. The boy's father admits his small faith, but asks Jesus to help him have more (9:24). Some people believe that without faith, miracles are impossible.

After the miracle the disciples asked Jesus why they had been unable to cast the evil spirit out of the boy. Jesus stated simply that prayer was needed (9:29), showing that the faith they needed was faith in God.

NOTE

EPILEPSY?
Some have argued that the boy's condition is very similar to a disorder of the nervous system called epilepsy. Epilepsy causes the sufferer to have fits, which may include foaming at the mouth and throwing their arms and legs around uncontrollably. They can then remain unconscious for about half an hour.

Some have argued that the boy in the story does in fact have epilepsy. At the time of Jesus it would have been mistaken for demonic possession.

The boy in Mark's account was also unable to speak, and Jesus addresses the spirit as a *"deaf and dumb spirit" (9:25),* suggesting the boy was also unable to hear. These conditions are not usually associated with epilepsy.

Even if the boy's condition was epilepsy this was a remarkable miracle. Even today there is no known cure for epilepsy.

IN A GROUP

'This story shows that people need to believe before miracles can happen.'

Do you agree or disagree? Give reasons for your answer showing that you have considered more than one point of view.

FOR YOUR FOLDER

1. What did Jesus find happening when he returned from the mountain after the Transfiguration?

2. What did the people at the time believe was wrong with the boy?

3. How might the boy's condition be explained today?

4. Why do you think the disciples had been unable to help the boy?

5. What can Christians learn from the attitude of the boy's father?

Chapter 4

THE KINGDOM OF GOD

THE COMING OF THE KINGDOM
MARK 1:14–18

When you hear the word 'kingdom' you might think of a geographical place. You might be reminded of fairy tales that you were told as a child, or think of a place like the United Kingdom.

When the Bible talks about the 'Kingdom of God' it doesn't refer to a geographical kingdom, or to a place somewhere up in the sky. Jesus' understanding of the Kingdom of God was that it was a group of people: those who regarded God as their king. When Jesus began his ministry in Galilee he preached using the words:

> *"the right time has come and the Kingdom of God is near! Turn away from your sins and believe the Good News!"*
> *(Mark 1:15)*

What Jesus meant was that God's rule or kingdom had come. As his ministry progressed Jesus taught his followers more about what this meant for their lives.

Immediately after this Jesus went on to call some of his disciples. Mark tells us that Simon and his brother Andrew, two fishermen, left their jobs behind and followed Jesus immediately.

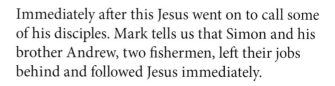

PARABLES

A parable is a story that illustrates a spiritual truth about the Kingdom of God. Jesus used parables to teach his followers.

Jesus' disciples asked him why he used parables when he talked to people. Jesus explained that through parables those who wanted to know more about God's kingdom would progress to understand more. Those who had closed their minds and their hearts to God would never understand even a little (4:10–12).

Jesus used parables to teach the people for the following reasons:

1. They were a common method used by many teachers or *rabbis* at that time.

2. A parable was easy to understand.

3. Parables challenged people to work out the meaning for themselves. People would have enjoyed listening and trying to discover the hidden meaning.

4. Jesus used everyday situations in his parables. It showed the people that he was on their level and understood their lives.

Allegories

Some of the parables told by Jesus are also classed as 'allegories'. An allegory is a type of parable where the characters and events in the story all represent real people and events. This means that every detail in the allegory has a meaning, unlike a parable which makes one simple point. An example of an allegory is the Parable of the Sower.

IN A GROUP

1. Discuss what the difference is between a parable and an allegory.

2. In pairs explain why parables were a popular teaching method.

NOTE

Jesus was a teacher (*rabbi*) who tried to get God's message across to the ordinary people. His teaching can be described as being both practical and challenging and he used relevant stories and themes to keep his audiences interested.

Jesus' teaching was not only relevant for the first century but can also be applied to life in the twenty-first century.

THE PARABLE OF THE SOWER   MARK 4:1–20

Jesus told three parables of growth. The first is the Parable of the Sower– a clear example of a parable or allegory about the Kingdom of God. It is one of the most famous parables told by Jesus.

Mark writes about this parable in three parts:

1. Chapter 4:1-9:
   The Parable of the Sower which Jesus told to a large crowd,

2. Chapter 4:10-12:
   Jesus explains the purpose of parables to his disciples,

3. Chapter 4:13-20
   Jesus explains the Parable of the Sower to his disciples.

As well as having meaning for the listeners of Jesus' day the Parable of the Sower has a clear message for people today.

The following diagram explains the meaning of the Parable of the Sower:

THE PARABLE	MEANING	SIGNIFICANCE FOR TODAY
"Once there was a man who went out to sow grain." (4:3)	**Man** God **Seed** The Word of God	The parable teaches what will happen when the Word of God is proclaimed. The Word of God is like seed which is planted and starts to grow. If people listen to God's word they will grow in a spiritual way.
"As he scattered the seed in the field some of it fell along the path and the birds ate it up." (4:4)	**Path and birds** "Some people are like the seeds that fall along the path; as soon as they hear the message, Satan comes and takes it away." (4:15)	Some people are distracted from taking the Christian faith seriously. Can you think of some things that might distract people?
"Some of it fell on the rocky ground, where there was little soil. The seeds soon sprouted, because the soil wasn't deep. But when the sun came up, it burnt the young plants; and because the roots had not grown deep enough, the plants soon dried up." (4:5–6)	**Rocky ground** "As soon as they hear the message, they receive it gladly. But it does not sink deep into them, and they don't last long." (4:16–17) **Sun** "So when trouble or persecution comes along because of the message, they give up at once." (4:18)	Some people are attracted by Christianity until they realise what it means to be a Christian, that it requires a deep commitment. **What sort of changes might someone have to make to be a Christian?**
"Some of the seed fell among the thorn bushes, which grew up and choked the plants." (4:7)	**Thorn bushes** "The ones who hear the message, but the worries about this life, the love for riches, and all other kinds of desires crowd in and choke the message, and they don't bear fruit." (4:18-19)	Some people let worries ruin God's influence on their lives. **What sort of worries might they have?** The 'thorns' can be compared to greed, anger or jealousy, all of which choke spiritual growth.
"But some seed fell in good soil, and the plants produced corn, some produced a hundred grains, others sixty, and others thirty." (4:8)	**Good soil** "They hear the message, accept it, and bear fruit: some thirty, some sixty, and some one hundred." (4:20)	A few people will accept the Gospel message and stay firm in their faith, in spite of difficulties which they may face. They will continue to grow as Christians, carrying out God's purpose in their lives.

IN A GROUP

1. Discuss the different ways in which people respond to the Gospel message today.

2. What distractions prevent people from becoming Christians?

THE LAMP ON A STAND
MARK 4:21–22

Oil lamps were used in homes to provide light at night. Jesus explained that you obviously did not put the lamps underneath a bowl or underneath a bed. Instead the lamp was put where it would provide the most light. So followers of Jesus were not to hide away. This may have been difficult for Mark's readers who were suffering under persecution. For today's readers, this parable teaches the importance of witnessing and sharing the Christian faith.

Some people think that this parable also criticises the religious leaders for hiding the truth of the Kingdom of God from the people.

THE PARABLE OF THE GROWING SEED
MARK 4:26–29

This is the second parable of growth, and it is found only in Mark's Gospel.

Have you ever planted something and been frustrated because you can't see it grow or don't understand how it grows? In this parable a farmer sows his seed in the ground and all he can do is wait until the harvest. He just has to get on with his business while the plants are growing.

There are a number of different ways this parable can be understood. Most simply, once the seed of the Word of God is sown, nobody knows how a person's faith grows within them.

Also Jesus' teaching will continue to spread and grow until the end of time when God will gather the harvest.

Mark's first readers were suffering persecution under the Romans. This parable would encourage them as they met with opposition and failure– though it is unseen, the Kingdom of God is coming.

THE PARABLE OF THE MUSTARD SEED
MARK 4:30–32

This is the third parable of growth. The mustard seed was a small seed but it grew into a huge plant, some as high as ten feet tall (three metres). The mustard plant in Jesus' story seems to grow unusually large.

Like the other parables of growth, Jesus emphasises how great things come from small beginnings. The Kingdom of God started small, but would grow and spread across the world.

Jesus mentions birds nesting in the branches of the plant. In Jewish Scripture birds sometimes represent the nations of the world (Ezekiel 31:6; Daniel 4:10-12). Jesus seems to be saying that the Kingdom of God will include people of other nations, not just Jews. This would have been important for Mark's readers, many of whom were not Jewish.

FOR YOUR FOLDER

1. Name the three parables of growth in Mark's Gospel.

2. Why do you think Jesus used nature in his parables?

3. How might the parable of the growing seed be interpreted?

4. Explain the meaning of the parable of the mustard seed.

5. 'The parables of growth teach that the Kingdom of God will come regardless of how Christians live their lives.' Do you agree or disagree? Give reasons for your answer.

JESUS AND THE CHILDREN   MARK 10:13–16

Mark shows particular concern for children by including this story. Mark does not tell us why the disciples were annoyed but it seems they were worried that Jesus might be bothered by people bringing their children for a blessing. Jesus was angry with the disciples for sending people away. Instead Jesus welcomed the children and blessed them, teaching:

> *"Whoever does not receive the Kingdom of God like a child will never enter it" (10:14).*

This has been interpreted to mean that followers of Jesus should show some of the qualities that young children have. This does not mean being childish or immature, but trusting and depending on God, just as children depend on adults.

FOR YOUR FOLDER

1. Why do you think the disciples tried to stop people bringing their children to Jesus?

2. Which childlike qualities do you think Jesus was suggesting his followers should have?

3. Do you think Christians today can learn anything from Jesus' attitude to children?

ENTRY INTO THE KINGDOM   MARK 10:17–31

IN A GROUP

What do you think it would be like to win the lottery?

What would you do with the money?

Would you still live in the same house or town?

Would you give money to your friends?

Where would you draw the line?

Think about how your life would change.

Would you be happier than you are now?

A man came to Jesus because he wanted to know what thing he should do to receive eternal life. Jesus told him to keep the Commandments and he listed some as examples: do not murder; do not steal; do not accuse anyone falsely; respect your father and mother. The man told Jesus that he had obeyed all the commandments. Jesus then told him he needed only one thing:

> *"…go and sell all you have and give the money to the poor, and you will have riches in heaven" (10:21).*

Imagine how the man felt! He obviously had a lot of money and possessions. The fact that he went away sad suggests that he wanted to follow Jesus but was unwilling to give up his wealth.

Jesus placed great importance on a person's attitude to money. He went on to tell his disciples:

> *"How hard it is to enter the Kingdom of God! It is much harder for a rich person to enter the Kingdom of God than for a camel to go through the eye of a needle"*
> *(10 24–25).*

Jesus uses this figure of speech to emphasise his point– it is almost impossible for the rich to enter the Kingdom of God (The saying 'eye of the needle' could refer to a small door in the city wall. The door was only large enough for a person, and a camel would never be able to fit through).

The disciples would have been stunned by this teaching. The people of this time looked upon riches as a blessing from God or a reward for good behaviour. The rich were always considered to have been favoured by God. If this was not the case then it seemed as if no one could be saved.

FOR YOUR FOLDER

1. **Name two things the man had to do to receive eternal life.**

2. **Why did the young man go away sad?**

3. **What comparison did Jesus make to show how difficult it would be for a rich person to enter the Kingdom of Heaven?**

4. **Why would the disciples find it hard to accept the idea that riches could stand in the way of entry into the kingdom?**

5. **What lessons about money and possessions can be learned from the attitude and teaching of Jesus?**

6. **Do you think the teaching of Jesus about money and possessions is relevant for Christians today?**

THE GREAT COMMANDMENT   MARK 12:28–34

The teachers of the Law, sometimes called Scribes, interpreted the Law of Moses and decided how it should be applied. On this occasion a teacher of the Law asked Jesus:

> *"Which commandment is the most important of all?" (12:28).*

Jesus answered him using two quotations from scripture. The first is from Deuteronomy 6:4-5. This is called the Shema - a daily prayer and the Jewish statement of faith:

> *"Listen Israel! The Lord our God is the only Lord. Love the Lord with all your heart, with all your soul, with all your mind, and with all your strength" (Mark 12:30).*

The second quotation is from Leviticus 19:18:

> *"Love your neighbour as you love yourself" (Mark 12:31).*

Jesus concludes:

> *"There is no other commandment more important than these two" (Mark 12:31).*

Unlike other teachers of the Law, this one was not trying to trick Jesus into saying something controversial. In fact he praised Jesus for his answer. Jesus acknowledged the wisdom of this teacher of the Law and told him that he was not far from the Kingdom of God. Mark shows us that not all religious leaders were against Jesus.

FOR YOUR FOLDER

1. What two commandments did Jesus say were the most important of all?

2. Why do you think Jesus told this teacher of the Law that he was not far from the Kingdom of God?

3. How do you think Christians can carry out the great commandment today?

4. 'Christians today don't do enough to love their neighbour.' Do you agree or disagree? Give reasons for your answer.

Chapter 5

THE DEATH AND RESURRECTION OF JESUS

The importance of Jesus' death and Resurrection to the Gospel writers is enormous. While only two of them (Matthew and Luke) record Jesus' birth, all four describe in detail the events surrounding Jesus' death and Resurrection. In Mark's Gospel three out of the sixteen chapters are taken up with what is known as the 'Passion narrative'.

The word *passion* originally means 'suffering'. The term 'passion of Christ' is commonly used at Easter time to describe the suffering Jesus endured.

Jesus' death was inevitable. However, it still brought immense sadness and distress to his followers. Looking back, Christians can celebrate that because of Jesus' death the offer of salvation is open to all people. It is interesting that Christianity is the only religion that actively celebrates its founder's death. Through Jesus' Resurrection he defeated the power of evil and death. Jesus' death and Resurrection are central to the Christian faith.

In this section we will look at the events surrounding the death and Resurrection of Jesus and consider their significance for Christians.

THE PLOT AGAINST JESUS   MARK 14:1–2

Opposition to Jesus had been building up for some time. Mark presents Jesus' enemies, the chief priests and the elders, as finalising the plot to kill him. They were wary of arresting Jesus during the Passover in case there was a riot. Many pilgrims from Galilee and the Diaspora were present in Jerusalem for the Passover.

JUDAS AGREES TO BETRAY JESUS
MARK 14:10–11

Judas Iscariot went to the chief priests to betray Jesus. Nobody knows why Judas decided to do this. Whatever the reason, Judas found his proposal was welcomed by the religious leaders. They promised to pay him for this and so he looked out for his opportunity to hand Jesus over to them.

FOR YOUR FOLDER

1. How many days before the Passover did the religious leaders meet to plot against Jesus?

2. Why were they reluctant to arrest Jesus during the Passover festival?

3. What was Judas promised in return for betraying Jesus?

4. Do you think Judas is responsible for beginning the chain of events that led to the death of Jesus? Give reasons for your answer.

THE PASSOVER MEAL AND THE LAST SUPPER

MARK 14:17–26

Every year Jews celebrate the Passover festival. It remembers the night the Israelites escaped from Egypt where they had been slaves (the Exodus). As Jesus was a Jew, he also celebrated the Passover every year. He had sent his disciples to make sure that everything was ready.

Jesus celebrated the Passover meal along with his disciples. Jesus suddenly announced that he would be betrayed by someone who was sitting at the table with him:

"One who dips his bread in the dish with me" (14:20).

All of the disciples expressed shock and each of them asked Jesus if they had somehow done something to betray him. Judas asked, *"Surely you don't mean me, do you?"*, but at this stage nobody knew who the traitor was because they had all dipped their bread in a common dish.

Jesus pointed out that the traitor would not escape God's judgement:

"It would have been better for that man if he had never been born" (14:21).

What happened next has become the most important ritual for Christians everywhere. Jesus took elements of the Passover meal and made them symbols of his death.

Following the usual format of the Passover meal, Jesus blessed the bread, broke it, and passed it around. He did the same with the wine. Jesus explained that the bread was his body and that the wine was his blood, which sealed God's covenant. Just as the previous covenants between people and God had been sealed with sacrifice, Jesus' death would be the final sacrifice enabling all people to receive God's blessing and forgiveness:

"This is my blood which is poured out for many, my blood which seals God's covenant." (14:23).

In verse 25 Jesus refers to a time in the future when they would meet again in God's Kingdom.

NOTE

Passover

The Passover or *Seder* meal which Jesus had with his disciples followed a set format:
– An opening prayer and a blessing of the cup
– The dipping of herbs in salt water
– The breaking of unleavened bread
– The reading of the story of the Passover
– The blessing of the second cup
– The festive meal of roast lamb
– The blessing of the third cup

Each item of food on the table symbolised what happened on the night of the first Passover when the Israelites escaped from Egypt. Jews today still celebrate the Passover.

At the Last Supper, Jesus used two of the items on the Passover table to symbolise his own forthcoming death. He took the unleavened bread and said *"this is my body"*. He also took the wine and said *"this is my blood"*. Christians today still remember that night by repeating the actions of eating bread and drinking wine. Different Christian traditions give this act of remembrance different names: Eucharist; Mass; The Lord's Supper; Holy Communion.

DIFFERENT UNDERSTANDINGS OF COMMUNION

Catholic Church	Protestant tradition
In the Catholic Church the Eucharist or Communion is celebrated daily in the **Mass**. Catholics believe that during the Eucharist the bread and wine change to become the body and blood of Christ. In other words, Christ becomes physically present in the bread and wine. This is known as **transubstantiation**.	In most Protestant churches, Communion is regarded as a memorial of Christ's death. The bread and wine do not change at all because they are simply symbols of what Christ has done. Communion means 'sharing' and at a Communion service Christians share together to remember the suffering and death of Christ.

FOR YOUR FOLDER

1. Describe the main events which took place during the Last Supper.

2. What new meaning did Jesus give to the bread and the wine?

3. Explain how communion is linked to the Passover meal.

4. Explain some differences in belief and practice for communion in Christian denominations today.

THE EVENTS AT GETHSEMANE AND JESUS' ARREST
MARK 14:32–50

The disciples went with Jesus to the Garden of Gethsemane, an olive tree plantation. His three closest disciples, Peter, James and John, who had been with him at the Transfiguration, went further into the garden with him while he prayed. Jesus was clearly distraught about what lay ahead:

> *"The sorrow in my heart is so great that it almost crushes me. Stay here and keep watch"* (14:34).

Jesus told Peter, James and John to keep watch, but even though they probably realised that something momentous was about to happen, they were not able to stay awake.

On this occasion Jesus' human nature and his divine nature are clearly seen. Jesus' humanity is shown in that he asked that the cup of suffering be taken away from him. This may have been a desperate plea for God to bring about his Kingdom without suffering being necessary. However, Jesus showed his divine nature in that he wanted to do God's will, even if that meant torture and death:

> *"Yet not what I want but what you want"* (14:36).

Jesus longed for his disciples to be close to him in his moments of suffering as he thought about what lay ahead. He asked them three times to stay awake and keep watch, but they kept falling asleep. He challenged Peter about this asking him if he could not even stay awake for an hour. Jesus knew they were exhausted but warned them not to fall into temptation:

> *"The spirit is willing but the flesh is weak"*
> *(14:38).*

The disciples did not appreciate the seriousness of what Jesus was going through. This meant that he had to cope with the mental suffering on his own.

The Significance of Gethsemane for Today

The events at the Garden of Gethsemane offer great comfort to Christians today when they are suffering things like bereavement or injustice. They believe that Jesus will understand what they are going through because he experienced so much suffering himself. Just like Jesus, Christians who suffer hand their problems over to God in prayer.

When Jesus prayed at Gethsemane he called God *abba*, which was a familiar term like 'daddy'. Many Christians feel that they can approach God like a loving father and talk to him about their problems.

The crowd arrested Jesus and one of those with Jesus drew his sword and cut off the ear of the High Priest's slave. Jesus allowed himself to be arrested but he asked them why they had come to take him by surprise at night, as if he were an outlaw.

The disciples were so shocked by what happened that they ran away.

Jesus knew that the time of his final suffering had come:

> *"The hour has come! Look the Son of Man is now being handed over to the power of sinners" (14:41).*

Judas arrived with the Chief Priests and elders, and an armed crowd to arrest Jesus. In order to make sure the right man was arrested Judas kissed Jesus on the cheek, a common greeting in that culture. He betrayed Jesus with an act of friendship. This makes Judas' betrayal even worse.

NOTE

Peter, James and John – the inner circle

Three of Jesus' disciples: Peter, James and John, stand out as having a special bond with Jesus. There are three occasions in Mark's Gospel where they alone are with Jesus to witness special events:

- The raising of Jairus' daughter from the dead (Ch.5:21–43)

- The Transfiguration (Ch.9:2–13)

- The events in the Garden of Gethsemane (Ch.14:32–42)

1. How did the disciples let Jesus down in Gethsemane?

2. What did Jesus mean when he said, *"The hour has come"*?

3. Pick out two phrases from Mark 14:32–50 which describe Jesus' sorrow.

4. Why did Judas kiss Jesus?

5. Why do you think the disciples left Jesus when he was arrested?

6. Do you think it helps if people can talk to God in the same way they approach a loving father? Give reasons for your answer, showing that you have considered other viewpoints.

IN A GROUP

Discuss the following questions:

1. What can Christians learn from the behaviour of the disciples in this story?

2. Do you think this story can bring comfort to people in times of suffering?

3. Explain why Jesus submitted peacefully to his arrest. As the Messiah, what else could he have done?

4. Can you think of any famous Christians whose faith has been tested? What happened and how did they overcome their time of testing?

JESUS BEFORE THE COUNCIL

MARK 14:53–65

The Sanhedrin was the official Jewish council or court of justice. It had 71 members, made up of Pharisees and Sadducees. The head of the council was the High Priest, who at the time of Jesus was Caiaphas.

The council was in control of the affairs of the Jewish people in Palestine. It had most of the powers of a normal court but was not allowed to carry out the death sentence. Only the Romans had the power to put someone to death.

Jesus was brought before the Sanhedrin on a charge of blasphemy, which means speaking in an offensive way about God. There were certain rules that had to be followed for a trial and it seems that Jesus' trial was carried out unfairly. For example:

- A court was not usually held in the High Priest's house. Jesus' trial took place in Caiaphas' house.

- Trials that could result in an execution could not take place at night. Jesus' trial was at night.

- False witnesses could be punished by death. At Jesus' trial two witnesses accused Jesus of threatening to destroy the Temple. (In John 2:19 Jesus told the Jewish authorities that if the Temple was torn down he would have the ability to rebuild it in three days. However, Jesus had not been talking about the real Temple but his body.)

At first Jesus did not answer this accusation, but when he was put under the oath and asked if he was the Messiah he replied: *"I am" (14:62).*

Jesus was careful not to agree with the High Priest's use of the word 'messiah', but went on to explain his identity in his own terms:

"You will all see the Son of Man seated on the right of the Almighty and coming with the clouds of heaven!" (14:62)

You will remember that 'Son of Man' is one of the titles that Jesus often used for himself. This time it refers to the prophecy of Daniel (Daniel 7:13).

The High Priest had heard enough and tore his robes to express his outrage at such blasphemy. Blasphemy was punishable by death by stoning according to the Jewish Law (Leviticus 24:16). The others attacked Jesus, spitting, punching and mocking him.

FOR YOUR FOLDER

1. What was the Sanhedrin?
2. Where was Jesus taken when he was arrested?
3. Explain the meaning of the term 'blasphemy'.
4. What accusation was brought against Jesus about the Temple?
5. Do you think Jesus was right to remain silent when questioned?
6. Why could the Sanhedrin not put Jesus to death?

JESUS BEFORE PILATE
MARK 15:1–20

Pilate, the Roman Governor, was the only one who could officially sentence Jesus to death, so the Jewish leaders handed him over for a second trial. Because blasphemy was not a crime under Roman law, it was twisted into a political charge. By saying that Jesus claimed to be the Messiah the Jewish leaders could argue that he was guilty of leading a rebellion against the Roman Empire.

Mark tells the story of Jesus before Pilate very quickly. It is not certain where the trial took place but it may have been in the fortress of Antonia (see map of Jerusalem on page 9).

Pilate's question to Jesus probably arose out of the Sanhedrin's report that Jesus had claimed to be the Messiah. When Jesus was brought before Pilate he asked him: *"Are you the King of the Jews?"*(15:2). Previously Herod the Great had been called the King of the Jews. If Jesus accepted the same title for himself it could be argued that he wanted to rule Palestine and overthrow the Romans.

Jesus replied *"So you say"* (15:2), but he did not say anything to the accusations made by the chief priests, which surprised Pilate and gave him no real reason to charge Jesus. Pilate realised that Jesus was a threat to the authority of the Sanhedrin, and they were trying to get rid of him. He was also aware that Jesus was very popular among the ordinary people.

In an attempt to find a simple solution, Pilate took the opportunity to use a Passover tradition. Every year the governor could set free one prisoner as a favour to the Jews. At the time there was a well known prisoner called Barabbas who had caused riots and was known to be a dangerous man. Pilate offered the crowd the choice of releasing either Jesus or Barabbas. It seemed obvious that the crowd would ask for Jesus to be released.

Pilate's plan backfired because the Sanhedrin persuaded the crowd to ask for Barabbas, a possible Zealot, to be released instead of Jesus.

Pilate's job was to maintain Roman rule in Palestine, and that meant keeping good relations with the local leaders. Pilate did what the crowd wanted and sent Jesus to be crucified.

FOR YOUR FOLDER

1. Describe the main features of Jesus' trial before Pilate.

2. Explain why Pilate may have had doubts about Jesus' guilt.

3. Explain some of the ways in which Jesus did not get a fair trial. You may use examples from the Jewish and Roman trials.

4. What can Christians learn from the suffering and behaviour of Jesus at his trials?

IN A GROUP

What sort of a person do you think Pilate was? Do you think he was responsible for the death of Jesus? Who else shared the blame?

FURTHER THINKING

'It is impossible to decide who was responsible for the death of Jesus'. Do you agree or disagree?

THE CRUCIFIXION AND DEATH OF JESUS
MARK 15:21-41

Crucifixions took place outside the city wall on a hill called *Golgotha*– 'the place of the skull'. Crucifixion was the most extreme form of Roman execution, reserved for the worst criminals. Jewish scripture described anyone who died by crucifixion as *"under God's curse"* (Deuteronomy 21:22–23). The place of Jesus' death symbolised rejection by people and by God.

Golgotha: Can you see why it is called the 'place of the skull'?

At that time it was not unusual to make a prisoner carry the cross-beam of their own cross to the site of the crucifixion. The fact that Jesus needed the assistance of a man from Cyrene to carry his cross probably shows that he was weak from the torture and beating he had received from the Roman soldiers (15:16–20).

The soldiers offered Jesus a drink – a kind of painkiller, which he refused. He was crucified between two criminals. The charge against each criminal would have been written at the top of their cross. In Jesus' case it would have read *IESUS NAZAREUS REX IUDAEORUM* – 'Jesus of Nazareth, King of the Jews' .

The Romans crucified people publicly as an example to others. Mark records that people gathered to watch and even shouted abuse at those condemned. The crowd laughed at Jesus' weakness and reminded him of his claims to have the power of God (*15:29-30*).

The religious leaders also hurled abuse at Jesus (*15:31-32*), as did the two who were crucified with him.

The prophet Isaiah had described the Messiah as a suffering servant:

"He was arrested and led off to die, and no one cared about his fate. He was put to death for the sins of our people" (Isaiah 53:8).

Mark here presents Jesus as that suffering servant, forsaken and rejected by everyone and yet, at the same time, fulfilling the prophecies about the Messiah.

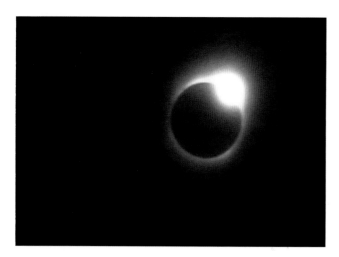

Mark records some strange and amazing things that happened during the last hours of Jesus' life. The whole region was covered in darkness, even though it was the middle of the day. In the Jewish scriptures darkness was often a symbol of tragedy or judgement (Exodus 10:21–23; Amos 8:9–10).

Jesus then called out the words of Psalm 22:1: *"Eloi Eloi, lema sabacthani"* which means "My God, my God, why did you abandon me?" Some people thought he was calling for the prophet Elijah who, it was believed, would help those in need.

Jesus cried out with a loud shout and died. It would have been unusual for someone so near to death to have the strength to do this. This may have been why the army officer was so convinced that Jesus was the Son of God (*15:39*).

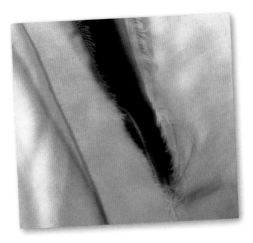

The curtain hanging in the Holy of Holies was torn in two, from top to bottom. This is a symbolic event:

The Holy of Holies was the part of the Temple where the presence of God was said to dwell (see page 16). It was separated from the rest of the temple by a thick curtain. Strict instructions were given concerning the location of this curtain:

"Make a curtain of fine linen woven with blue, purple and red wool. Embroider it with figures of winged creatures. Hang it on four posts of acacia wood covered with gold, fitted with hooks, and set in four silver bases…The curtain will separate the Holy Place from the Most Holy Place" (Exodus 26:31–33).

Only the High Priest could pass through the curtain into God's presence, once a year, having performed complex rituals in preparation.

If the curtain had been torn by human hands the tear would have begun at the bottom. Mark records that the curtain was torn from *"top to bottom"* (15:37) which suggests that God himself tore the curtain. The destruction of the curtain, which symbolically separated people from God, represented that the way to God was now open. All people could now come before God.

The dead being raised to life represented the future for all those who trusted in Christ's death as a sacrifice which would bring them forgiveness.

Mark draws attention to the presence of the women who watched the crucifixion from a distance (15:40–41). They did not run away like the disciples. These same women stayed at the cross and were the first at the tomb (16:1), which shows how devoted they were to Jesus. Mark even identifies them by name (15:40).

IN A GROUP

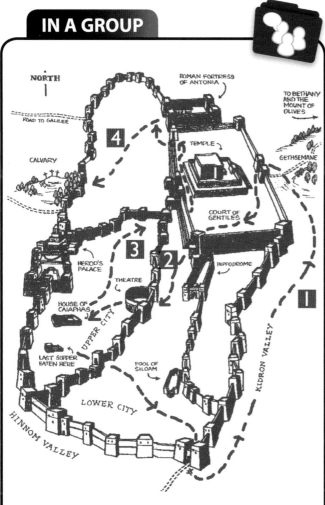

Use the references below and the map above to follow Jesus' movements through Jerusalem before his death.

Mark 14:26

Mark 14:53

Mark 15:1, 16

Mark 15:22

FOR YOUR FOLDER

1. Why would the events of the last week of Jesus' life have been a difficult time for the disciples?

2. Jesus was crucified at Golgotha. What is the meaning of 'Golgotha'?

3. What part did Simon of Cyrene play in the events leading up to the crucifixion?

4. What was Jesus saying when he cried out 'Eloi, Eloi, lema sabacthani'?

5. What did the Roman soldier say after Jesus' death?

6. Why is the death of Jesus important for Christians?

7. If Jesus was a good man, and the 'Son of God' why was he put to death?

THE BURIAL OF JESUS   MARK 15:42-47

The account of the burial of Jesus is important because it shows that Jesus was really dead. A man from Arimathea, called Joseph, asked Pilate for the body of Jesus so that he could bury him in a tomb. He is described as being a respected member of the Council, which probably means the Sanhedrin. It is not clear whether Joseph was a public follower of Jesus, but Mark describes him as someone who was waiting for the coming of the Kingdom of God (15:42-43).

As a Jew he would have been wary about coming in contact with a dead body, especially that of a criminal – this would have made him unclean, and unable to take part in religious activities. Corpses from crucifixions were usually burned at the town dump, but Joseph obviously wanted Jesus to have a proper burial. He risked severe punishment by approaching Pilate. This shows the love and respect he had for Jesus.

Mark explains how Pilate checked with the soldiers to make sure Jesus was dead before releasing the body. Joseph laid the body of Jesus in the tomb and rolled a stone in front of the entrance. Mary Magdalene and the other Mary sat close by and watched.

FOR YOUR FOLDER

1. Who was Joseph of Arimathea?
2. Why do you think he may have wanted to bury Jesus?
3. What precautions did Pilate take before releasing the body to Joseph?
4. Who watched the burial?

JESUS' RESURRECTION   MARK 16:1-8

Out of all the Gospel writers Mark's account of the Resurrection is the shortest.

Early on the Sunday morning Mary Magdalene, Mary the mother of James, and Salome returned to the tomb to anoint the body. They worried about how they could get the stone moved but when they got there someone had already rolled it away from the entrance to the tomb.

They entered the tomb and were alarmed to find a young man dressed in white. He told them that Jesus had risen and to go and tell the disciples and Peter to meet him in Galilee.

The women were terrified and ran out, telling no one of their experience because they were so afraid.

Some copies of Mark's Gospel finish at this point. It is a strange ending, emphasising the shock and strange feelings experienced by the women at the tomb. Other Gospels contain more information about Jesus appearing to the disciples, and some copies of Mark contain a summary of these stories (16:9-20).

IN A GROUP

1. **Who was responsible for the death of Jesus?**

   Traditionally the Jewish leaders have been blamed for the death of Jesus. The Gospels stress the part they played, even though the final decision was made by the Romans. Other people also played significant roles in the events leading up to Jesus' death.

   Look at the following list of people and write a sentence on the part they played in the death of Jesus:

The disciples	Pilate
Judas	The crowd
The Jewish leaders	Herod
Caiaphas	God
Jesus himself	

   Write a paragraph on who you think was most responsible for the death of Jesus.

2. **"Save yourself if you are God's Son."**

   Do you think Jesus should have avoided crucifixion? Discuss in small groups.

FOR YOUR FOLDER

1. What did the women see and experience when they returned to the tomb on the Sunday morning?

2. Explain the significance of Jesus' appearance to the women.

3. What would the Resurrection have meant to the disciples?

IN A GROUP

'The importance of Jesus' death and Resurrection for Christians cannot be underestimated. The two events go hand in hand and are the basis of the Christian faith.'

1. Look at the following reasons given and place them in order, starting with the reason that you think is most important:

   • Jesus' death and Resurrection shows that God can defeat the powers of evil, even death itself.

   • Jesus' death and Resurrection prove that Jesus was who he claimed to be – the promised Messiah.

   • Jesus' crucifixion changed the way people relate to God. The way is now open between people and God.

   • The Resurrection shows that there is life after death. This gives hope of everlasting life. Christians believe that they, too, will have life after death.

   • Jesus paid the price for people's sin.

2. Do you think that Jesus' death is more important for Christians today than his Resurrection?

CLASS DEBATE:
Did the Resurrection really happen?

- 'Belief in the physical resurrection of Jesus is difficult in the twenty-first century.'
  Do you agree or disagree? Give reasons for your answer.

- Most Christians accept that the Resurrection of Jesus was a real event. However, there is an ongoing debate about whether or not the Resurrection really happened or if it was just a symbolic event. In groups discuss the following theories that have been put forward. See if you can fill in any information in the missing boxes.

ARGUMENTS AGAINST	ARGUMENTS FOR
Jesus did not die but was only unconscious. The coolness of the tomb helped him revive and he got out of it with the help of the disciples.	If this was true, then what happened to Jesus?
Jesus did die but the disciples stole the body and then made up the story of the Resurrection to convince people that Jesus was alive.	After the Resurrection the disciples were prepared to risk torture and death for their faith. This is hard to believe if the Resurrection had just been a trick.
Jesus did die but the followers of Jesus, in their distress, hallucinated because they wanted to believe that Jesus had risen.	The authorities were not able to produce the body to prove them wrong.
The women failed to see the body of Jesus at the tomb because they went to the wrong tomb.	

IN A GROUP

Discuss:

Does it matter whether the Resurrection of Jesus really happened or not?

Would it be enough for Jesus to live on through his teachings? Consider 1 Corinthians 15.12–19.

Chapter 6

THE ROLE AND NATURE OF CHRISTIAN DISCIPLESHIP

All rabbis or teachers in Jesus' day had disciples who learned from their teaching and tried to follow in their footsteps. Jesus was no exception. He had twelve close followers or disciples who helped him in his ministry.

Jesus demanded total commitment from his disciples. Through his teaching he clearly stated that God should be first in their lives, above everything else. In the examples we will be studying it is clear that Jesus' disciples had a lot to learn and at times they had great difficulty in understanding what they were being taught. Christians today also see themselves as disciples of Jesus and try to live as closely as possible to his teaching.

Discipleship

A disciple is a follower or a learner. For example, in the world of work, a person might be a trainee mechanic who learns his trade from a fully qualified mechanic. This is called an apprenticeship.

Jesus' disciples made sacrifices to follow him. To be a Christian today also requires sacrifice. Some of the sacrifices a person might have to make in committing to Christianity include the following:

Attitudes towards money and possessions
"Can you have a lot of money and be a Christian?"

Service to others
"What should I do to help others?"

Friendships
"Who am I spending my time with?'

Priorities
"What are the most important things in my life?"

Popularity
"Am I prepared to give up my popularity?"

Comfortable lifestyle
"I have a great lifestyle. I'm not prepared to make any changes to follow Christ."

FURTHER THINKING

What sacrifices might someone have to make if they followed Christ?

JESUS CALLS HIS DISCIPLES

Jesus calls the fishermen
MARK 1:14-20

Simon and his brother Andrew were fishermen. When Jesus said to them *"come with me" (1:17),* he was asking them to leave their jobs. As he saw them catching fish, Jesus told them *"I will teach you to catch people"(1:17)* meaning that he would teach them how to bring people back to God.

Mark is interested in how these men responded to the call. Notice that they dropped everything to follow Jesus, and that they responded immediately. James and John responded in a similar way. They leave not only their jobs, but their father too *(1:20).*

Simon was later given the nickname *Peter* by Jesus, which means 'rock'. He was to become one of Jesus' closest disciples.

Jesus calls Levi
MARK 2:13-17

Levi was a tax collector. Remember that tax collectors were hated because they were dishonest and worked for the Romans (see page 13). Jesus' actions here would have horrified the Jewish religious leaders. As far as they were concerned Levi was a sinner and an outcast, yet Jesus called him to be one of his disciples. Like Simon and Andrew, Levi responded immediately to the call of Jesus.

It seems that a celebration followed in the form of a meal at Levi's house. Friends of Levi's, also tax collectors, were present. This angered the Jewish religious leaders. According to Jewish Law, a Jew could not associate with outcasts like tax collectors as they were considered 'unclean'. This did not mean physical dirtiness, but religious impurity. By eating with such people Jesus was in danger of breaking the ritual laws.

The Pharisees asked Jesus' disciples, *"Why does he eat with such people?"(2:16).* Outcasts included those with skin diseases (lepers), prostitutes, criminals and tax collectors. Jesus' reply showed that, unlike most religious teachers, he was more concerned with helping the outcasts in society than keeping religious duties. To help everyone to understand this, Jesus used an everyday example – doctors are not needed for those who are in good health, but for the sick.

FOR YOUR FOLDER

1. What different types of people did Jesus include in his team of disciples?

2. Explain why the religious leaders were angry with the celebration at Levi's house?

3. What can Christians learn today from Jesus' choice of disciples?

FURTHER THINKING

Jesus did not go to these people because they received him warmly but because they needed him. How could this apply today?

JESUS' ATTITUDE TO THE SABBATH

MARK 2:23-28

At the time of Jesus the Oral Law listed actions and activities that were not allowed to take place on the Sabbath. The only exception to these laws was if someone's life was in danger.

One Sabbath Jesus' disciples were picking corn as they walked through the fields. The Pharisees saw this as one of the 39 actions that were forbidden on the Sabbath. The Pharisees challenged Jesus, saying *"It is against our Law for your disciples to do that on the Sabbath!" (2:24).*

Jesus told a story about King David in reply. The Jews considered David to be their greatest King and held him with high regard. However, Jesus reminded them that David had broken the Law for the sake of his men who were hungry. They ate the bread that was reserved for the priests *(1 Samuel 21).*

Jesus' attitude to the Sabbath is summed up in Mark 2:27:

> *"The Sabbath was made for the good of human beings; they were not made for the Sabbath".*

Jesus was saying that human need is more important than the Law. Jesus continued,

> *"So the Son of Man is Lord even of the Sabbath" (2:28).*

This was a controversial statement to make to the Pharisees. It seems that Jesus was saying he had the authority to do whatever he liked on the Sabbath.

FOR YOUR FOLDER

1. Explain why the actions of the disciples made the Pharisees angry.

2. Give an account of the story of David that Jesus used in his reply.

JESUS CHOOSES THE TWELVE   MARK 3:13-19

The word 'disciple' means 'one who learns'. 'Apostle' means 'messenger'. Jesus chose twelve apostles who would learn from him and carry out his work. The number twelve was significant because it represented the twelve tribes of Israel in the Jewish Scriptures.

The twelve were called to do three things:
- To be with Jesus (Jesus valued the importance of friendship),
- To be sent out to preach,
- To drive out demons.

The twelve apostles were:
1. Simon Peter
2. James (son of Zebedee and brother of John)
3. John (son of Zebedee and brother of James)
4. Andrew (the brother of Simon Peter)
5. Philip
6. Bartholomew
7. Matthew (a tax collector also called 'Levi')
8. Thomas
9. James (son of Alphaeus)
10. Thaddaeus (Judas, son of James)
11. Simon (the Zealot)
12. Judas Iscariot

How are Christians called to carry out God's work today?

Two people describe how they were led to carry out God's work:

Steve Stockman is a Presbyterian minister, who is chaplain at Queen's University Belfast. Steve is also a regular contributor to BBC Radio Ulster and author of **'Walk On; The Spiritual Journey of U2'** which is now translated into seven languages!

Steve talks about what he thinks it means to be called by God in the twenty-first century:

"I believe that first of all I am called by God to be 'me'. As a Christian it is important to discover your calling in life, so that you can help bring about God's Kingdom here on Earth. Your role is just as important whether you are called to work behind the till at your local supermarket or called to be a minister. Every Christian is called to be a witness to Christ.

"Frederick Buechner, who is a Presbyterian minister and novelist, says that vocation (calling) should be 'where your deepest gladness meets the world's greatest need.'

"I believe I was given the gift of communication. This is what drew me to become a Presbyterian minister. It is no more important than other vocations but it is where my deepest gladness meets the world's deepest need.

"I believe that through prayer and talking to others you can find out what God is calling you to do with your life. Then, by doing and getting on with it, if you experience a sense of fulfillment and deep gladness, you will know you are in the right place."

Father John is the parish priest in a small country Catholic parish:

"I came to an awareness of vocation (call) on three levels: creative, emotional and spiritual. However, it wasn't until I left school that I made the decision that I might become a priest. The seeds were sown years before.

"I had been in the Cathedral Choir and it was there that I developed a love of music – all sorts really, from Pop music to Classical. I really liked the music of the 'old' church. For a long time I couldn't decide between a career as a musician or as a priest. I found out that I could combine the two as a priest with a ministry in music. I use music as a way to reach out to people.

"The desire to become a priest was even deeper on the emotional and spiritual levels. I came from what would now be called a 'dysfunctional' family. Alcoholism was the problem. During my teenage years this really upset me. I received a lot of help and support from the priests at my boarding school. They were the only people I could turn to for advice and guidance. The memory of that stayed with me all these years and I think it was through their openness and influence that I have been able to help people in similar situations."

IN A GROUP

Explain how Steve and Father John were influenced to take up full time Christian work.

Make a list of the type of work that each of them might carry out as part of their ministry.

FOR YOUR FOLDER

1. Explain the meaning of the words 'apostle' and 'disciple'.

2. What three things did Jesus expect of his apostles?

3. Why do you think Jesus chose twelve disciples?

THE CHALLENGE OF WITNESSING
MARK 6:1-6

Jesus visited Nazareth, the place where he was brought up. Mark describes his experience there as very different from his stay in other places. The people of Nazareth did not recognise the importance of Jesus. They knew his family well. As far as they were concerned he was simply a carpenter, yet here he was preaching to them.

Jesus explained why the people of Nazareth rejected him:

> *"Prophets are respected everywhere except in their own home town and by their relatives and their family" (6:4)*

Mark tells us that Jesus was not able to carry out many miracles in Nazareth because of the people's lack of faith. The rejection by friends and family at Nazareth was a foretaste of the rejection that Jesus would face at the end of his life.

FOR YOUR FOLDER

1. Explain why it would have been difficult for the people of Nazareth to accept the authority of Jesus.

2. What does this story teach about faith?

3. How might this story influence Christians in how they spread the good news?

4. *'Prophets are respected everywhere except in their own home town and by their relatives and their family'* Do you think this is true? Can you think of any modern day examples?

THE MISSION OF THE TWELVE
MARK 6:7-13

The mission of the twelve marked a new stage in Jesus' ministry. The disciples were invited to join in Jesus' mission. The event is described in all three Synoptic Gospels.

Mark describes how the twelve were gathered together and sent out in pairs to do what they had seen Jesus do. Jesus gave them authority and power to cast out evil spirits and to heal the sick. The mission of the disciples is an extension of the mission of Jesus.

There were two main reasons why the disciples were sent out in pairs:

1. For protection – the roads would have been dangerous for a man to travel on his own.

2. It was accepted that the evidence of two witnesses could be trusted (Deuteronomy 17:6).

The disciples were given some further instructions. They were to travel light and rely on the hospitality of people who took them in. By doing so the disciples would show that they completely relied on God for everything that they would need. Being a disciple of Jesus means learning to depend on God rather then yourself.

Jesus expected his disciples to face rejection as well as acceptance. If the disciples were not welcomed in a town, they were told to shake the dust from their feet as they left – a warning to people that they had rejected God. Normally, Jews would shake the dust from their feet when leaving a Gentile area. For a Jew to give this symbolic gesture to another Jew was a very serious action.

Mark also includes the detail that the disciples anointed people with oil and they were healed. Olive oil was often used to heal at the time of Jesus. Oil is still used in some churches today for the anointing the sick.

NOTE

AN EXAMPLE OF MISSION IN ACTION:
Mother Teresa became a Loretto nun when she was 17 years old. She trained in Dublin and then went to Calcutta in India, where she taught in a school. She was very concerned about the amount of poverty she saw on the streets of India. She got permission from the Pope to go to help the poor. In 1950 she was allowed to form a new order and invited other nuns to come and join her in her work.

FURTHER THINKING

1. Find out how Mother Teresa spent the rest of her life from 1950 onwards.

2. Why do you think Mother Teresa helped the elderly, sick and poor?

3. What can other Christians learn from the work of Mother Teresa?

IN A GROUP

1. Have you ever come across people who work in pairs to spread their beliefs? Perhaps someone has called to your house or gives out leaflets in your town centre. How are these people treated by those that they meet?

2. What do you think of their methods of spreading their beliefs?

3. Can you think of other ways that people can share their faith in the twenty-first century?

4. Do you think that the Church today has a role to play in healing the sick?

FOR YOUR FOLDER

1. What did Jesus suggest that his followers should be prepared to do?

2. What advice did Jesus give to the twelve disciples when he sent them out on mission?

3. How were the disciples sent out and what authority did Jesus give them?

4. 'Being a disciple of Jesus is difficult in the twenty-first century.' Do you agree or disagree? Give reasons for your answer.

THE COST OF BEING A DISCIPLE
MARK 8:34-38

This teaching highlights the extent of the commitment Jesus expected from his followers. Being a true disciple of Jesus would require self-denial. Committed Christians must be willing to face even death for the sake of the Gospel:

> *"If anyone wants to come with me... he must forget self, carry his cross, and follow me."* (8:34)

It was a Roman custom for a person facing crucifixion to carry part of their own cross. It publicly showed the person submitting to the rule he had opposed. In the same way Christians had to publicly show that they submitted to Christ's authority.

For Mark's readers, under Roman persecution, the idea of suffering for their faith was a present reality. Many were killed for their belief in Christ. The suffering endured by these Christians is an example of how some people were prepared to 'carry their cross'. In other words they knew they might die for their faith but still they remained faithful to Christ.

Some Christians today also face the possibility of death for their faith; others may simply suffer mockery or loss of friends. Either way, to be a Christian usually involves some sort of sacrifice.

Mark highlighted that there was a reward for those who would be committed to Jesus:

> *"For whoever wants to save his own life will lose it; but whoever loses his life for me and for the gospel will save it"* (8:35)

Mark also pointed out that those who were ashamed of Jesus' teaching would be rejected by the Son of Man at the end of time (8:38).

FOR YOUR FOLDER

1. Jesus said *"If anyone wants to come with me... he must forget self, carry his cross, and follow me."* Give two examples of how a Christian may be asked to do this.

2. What do you think is most difficult about the Christian way of life?

3. What sort of dangers may the first followers of Jesus have faced?

IN A GROUP

'It is more difficult for teenagers to be true followers of Jesus today than it was for the first disciples'

Do you agree or disagree? Give reasons for your answer showing that you have considered more than one point of view.

FURTHER THINKING

Use the internet or a library to find out about St Francis of Assisi. He is an example of someone who lived a life of poverty and preaching.

Discuss what this kind of sacrifice might mean for Christians today.

JESUS AT THE TEMPLE
MARK 11:15-19

Jesus and the disciples arrive in Jerusalem, and Jesus goes to the Temple (refer back to pages 15–16 for information on the Temple). The Temple courts would have been bustling with Jews and God-fearing Gentiles who had travelled there to worship and make sacrifice.

Before an animal could be offered for sacrifice it had to be inspected by the Temple officials to make sure it was pure. The Temple courts were full of traders selling animals for sacrifice at ten or fifteen times more than the normal price.

Similarly, offerings of money were only acceptable in special coins. Roman coins, which carried an image of Caesar, were not acceptable. Money had to be changed into Galilean shekels or special Temple coins. The money changers charged a large fee for this service.

Jesus was outraged that people coming to worship God were being exploited like this. He overturned the tables of the money-changers and drove them out of the Temple.

Jesus quotes the prophet Isaiah:

"My Temple will be called a house of prayer for the people of all nations" (Isaiah 56:7).

He accuses the people, saying:

"You have turned it into a hideout for thieves!" (Mark 11:17).

Mark highlights the reaction of the religious leaders to Jesus' outburst. It was predicted that the Messiah would cleanse the Temple (Malachi 3:1–4). By his actions, Jesus was fulfilling prophecy.

COPING WITH TEMPTATION
MARK 9:42-50

In these verses Jesus gives some frightening warnings to emphasise the importance of faith. He talks about the seriousness of destroying the faith of children or those who are young in their faith. Jesus said:

"It would be better for that person to have a large millstone tied round his neck and be thrown into the sea" (9:42).

NOTE

A millstone was a large, heavy stone that was used to grind corn. Usually, millstones were so large that they had to be moved by animals.

Jesus warned his disciples to remove anything that might cause them to lose faith. He used strong imagery:

> *"If your hand makes you lose faith, cut it off!" (9:43).*

Jesus was stressing that life in the Kingdom of God is more important than anything, even the body.

"pay the Emperor what belongs to the Emperor, and pay God what belongs to God." (12:17)

Jesus avoided their trap and made a point about attitudes to Roman rule. The people may give money to the Romans, since it is Roman money anyway, but the people's loyalty should be to God.

FOR YOUR FOLDER

1. What warning did Jesus give about destroying the faith of children?

2. Explain how Jesus advises his followers to cope with temptation.

THE QUESTION ABOUT PAYING TAXES
MARK 12:13-17

Jesus' opponents were determined to trap him into saying something controversial that would make him unpopular or get him into trouble with the authorities.

They asked Jesus if the Law allowed them to pay taxes to the Roman Emperor. If Jesus said no, he would associate himself with the Zealot revolutionaries and then he could be arrested for speaking against Rome. If Jesus said yes he would seem to support Roman rule and would become very unpopular with the ordinary people.

Jesus did not give them an answer straight away. Instead he asked them to bring him a coin. Jesus drew their attention to the Emperor's head which was engraved on the coin. Then he told them:

FOR YOUR FOLDER

1. How did the Pharisees try to trick Jesus?

2. What do you think this story teaches about behaviour towards the government?

IN A GROUP

On this occasion Jesus was being drawn into a conversation about his attitude towards the Roman government.

Do you think religion and politics should be kept separate? Give reasons for your answer.

THE WIDOW'S OFFERING

MARK 12:41-44

Jesus is in the Temple once more and uses what he sees to teach his disciples about giving. They watched many rich men dropping large sums of money into the temple treasury, and then a poor widow dropped in two small coins.

Jesus teaches that the woman's act of giving was greater than that of the rich. The poor were thought of as unimportant compared to the rich. As a widow, this woman would have no source of income. The small amount of money was all she had, and yet she offered it to God.

It is clear that the sacrifice involved in giving is more important than the amount given. Jesus' disciples then and now are encouraged to offer all they have to God.

FOR YOUR FOLDER

1. Explain why Jesus praised the poor widow.
2. What lessons can Christians today learn from this story?

FURTHER THINKING

Find out what the temple treasury was used for.

THE PRESSURE OF DISCIPLESHIP

One of the pressures of being a follower of Jesus comes in the form of peer pressure. It may be easy to say you are a Christian if everyone else around you believes the same thing, but it is a different matter if faced with someone who ridicules you for your faith. Mark's first readers faced not only ridicule for their beliefs, but torture and death. Some people might find that they want to keep their heads down and not admit their beliefs.

Jesus predicts Peter's denial
MARK 14:26–31

In this passage Jesus makes three predictions. Firstly, he explained how his followers would be scattered after he dies. Secondly, he predicted that he would rise again. This should have completely amazed the disciples but it seems they did not register its significance. Their attention was on his third prediction: that Peter would deny knowing Jesus three times:

> *"I tell you that before the cock crows twice tonight, you will say three times that you do not know me." (14:30)*

Peter confidently shrugged off the suggestion that he could be disloyal and said he would never deny that he was a follower of Jesus. He even argued that he would be prepared to die with Jesus and the rest of the disciples said they would face death too.

Peter denies Jesus
MARK 14:66–72

It was not long before Jesus' prediction about Peter came true. During Jesus' trial before the Sanhedrin Peter was waiting outside in a courtyard. He was approached by several people who suggested that they had seen him with Jesus.

FURTHER THINKING

John's Gospel records a conversation between Jesus and Peter that takes place after the Resurrection (John 21:1–19).

Why do you think neither Jesus nor Peter mention Peter's denial?

What is Jesus asking Peter to do?

The first person who accused him was one of the High Priest's servant women. The woman repeats her claim to the bystanders. Finally, the bystanders accused him, recognising him as a Galilean. On all three occasions he denied it, as Jesus had predicted. It was only when he heard a cock crowing that he remembered what Jesus had said and he broke down and cried.

NOTE

WHAT HAPPENED TO PETER?

The book of Acts shows Peter leading the followers of Jesus, and spreading the good news about Jesus across the world. Peter also wrote two letters in his role as leader of the Church in Rome (1 Peter and 2 Peter). Some early writers refer to Mark's Gospel as 'The Memoirs of Peter', suggesting that the writer Mark wrote down the events as Peter witnessed them.

According to tradition, Peter died in his sixties – killed under Roman persecution, crucified upside-down.

FOR YOUR FOLDER

1. What did Jesus say the disciples would do before the night was over?

2. What was Peter's response to the suggestion that he might deny Christ?

3. When Jesus was being tried before the Sanhedrin what happened to Peter as he waited outside?

4. Explain the significance of the cock crowing.

5. Why do you think Peter denied Christ?

6. What might tempt Christians today to deny Christ?

7. *'The pressures facing Christians today are much more difficult than those faced by the first disciples.'* Do you agree or disagree?

St. Peter's Basilica in the Vatican, built on the site where Peter is believed to be buried.

IN A GROUP

How might Peter's behaviour be reassuring for Christians today?

Index

Acknowledgements

Author's acknowledgements

Thanks are due to a number of people who contributed to this book: Sam Smith from the Leprosy Mission, Father John and Steve Stockman.

Special thanks goes to Donna Finlay (CCEA); Joan Williams (CCEA); Philip Barnes (CCEA); Sheila Johnston and Michael Spence at Colourpoint for their thorough guidance throughout the editing process; Martin, Tom and Kate for their patience.

Picture credits

Cover image: iStockphoto

iStockphoto: 5, 9 (top right), 11, 12 (both), 13 (middle), 14 (bottom two), 19, 21 (both), 23, 24 (both), 25 (right), 27, 28, 29, 30, 32 (both), 33, 34 (both), 35 (left), 36, 37 39, 42, 44, 45, 46, 47, 48, 50, 51 (top), 54, 56, 57, 58 (both), 60 (right), 61, 64 (left), 66, 67 (left).

Alex Eleon: 9 (bottom right)
Masqueraid: 15 (left)
Gugganij: 22
Rick Pelleg: 41
Michael Spence: 51 (bottom right), 52 (top right)
Oliver Ren: 52 (left)
Steve Stockman: 60 (left)
Günter Rapp: 64 (right)

Copyright information

The logo of the Leprosy Mission (page 31) appears by kind permission of the organisation.

The following images are licensed under the GNU Free Documentation License. Permission is granted to copy, distribute and/or modify these documents under the terms of the GNU Free Documentation License, Version 2.1 or any later version published by the Free Software Foundation; with no Invariant Sections, no Front-Cover Texts and no Back-Cover Texts. A copy of the license can be viewed at http://www.fsf.org/licensing/licenses/fdl.html

Page 15 (bottom left) retrieved from http://upload.wikimedia.org/wikipedia/commons/e/e0/Ruins_of_the_Ancient_Synagogue_at_Bar%27am.jpg

Page 22 retrieved from http://upload.wikimedia.org/wikipedia/commons/2/2e/Banias_Spring_Cliff_Pan%27s_Cave.JPG